AURUM

FABIAN HARTMANN
HENNING STRASSBURGER
09-12-2011 — 10-02-2012

D0895799

ARTARY

ARTARY GALERIE DE-70182 Stuttgart
T. +49 (0)711 91260895 | F. +49 (0)711 91260896 | info@artary.de | www.artary.de
Tuesday – Friday 12 - 6 pm, Saturday 12 - 4 pm

Förderer der Ausstellung:

hessische
kultur
stiftung    KULTURAMT
STADT FRANKFURT AM MAIN

Mit großzügiger Unterstützung von:
Gagosian Gallery, London
Yvon Lambert, Paris
Galerie Eva Presenhuber, Zürich

Douglas
Gordon

19.11.2011
— 25.3.2012

www.mmk-frankfurt.de

MMK MUSEUM FÜR MODERNE KUNST
FRANKFURT AM MAIN

KATE WATERS
THE AIR THAT I BREATHE
DECEMBER 9 - JANUARY 29, 2011-2012
CATALOGUE AVAILABLE

GALERIE VOSS

Mühlengasse 3
40213 Düsseldorf

T +49 (0) 211 134982
F +49 (0) 211 133400

info@galerievoss.de
www.galerievoss.de

F.C. Gundlach, Brigitte Bauer, Op Art-Badeanzug von Sinz, Vouliagmeni/Griechenland 1966, © F.C. Gundlach

VANITY
FASHION / PHOTOGRAPHY FROM
THE F.C. GUNDLACH COLLECTION
October 21, 2011 – February 12, 2012

NO FASHION,
PLEASE!
PHOTOGRAPHY BETWEEN
GENDER AND LIFESTYLE
November 10, 2011 – January 22, 2012

KUNSTHALLE wien

Museumsplatz 1, 1070 Vienna
Infoline +43-1- 52189-33
www.kunsthallewien.at

Open Files

Studio Visits

Research

Featuring interviews with and images by:
Maurizio Anzeri, Lauren DiCioccio
Maria Ikonomopoulou , Inge Jacobsen
Shaun Kardinal, Stacey Page
Ehren Elizabeth Reed, Hinke Schreuders
Berend Strik, Melissa Zexter

IV

Meetings

V

Making

VI

Travelling: Zurich

Text & Interviews by
Corinne Olejak & Marc Valli
Photography by Dejan Savic

Galerie Hubert Winter

BIRGIT JÜRGENSSEN
Cyanotypes from 1988/89

January 10 - February 4, 2012

Breite Gasse 17   1070 Vienna   Austria   ph +43 1 5240976 (fax+9)
office@galeriewinter.at   www.galeriewinter.at
www.birgitjuergenssen.com

MARKUS PRACHENSKY
2.12.11–28.1.12

*Nicht Anonymität des Künstlers, nicht Kollektiv der Idee,
nicht intellektuelle Berechnung oder para-technische Erfindung,
nicht ein antiseptischer Abzug sind gefordert,
sondern wirkliche Malerei mit allen Höhen und Tiefen des Lebens
und der Spiritualität – enfin „retournons à la peinture".*

Markus Prachensky (1932 – 2011), „Manifest der Malerei", 1961

:galeriefreihausgasse

villach

Galerie der Stadt Villach
9500 Villach, Freihausgasse
T +43 (0) 42 42 / 205 - 3450
E dolores.hibler@villach.at, www.villach.at
Mo-Fr 10-12.30 u. 15-18, Sa 10-12
sundays and public holidays closed

Editor-in-chief
Marc Valli
marc@elephantmag.com
marcvalli@frameweb.com

Editors
Ana Ibarra
ana@frameweb.com

Margherita Dessanay
ma@frameweb.com

Katya Tylevich

Contributing Editors
Corinne Olejak, Astrid Stavro,
Joseph Wood, Natasha Hoare

Proofing
Karla Hammer

We would like to particularly
thank everyone in Zurich for their
invaluable help.

For all editorial enquiries:
Elephant Magazine
c/o Magma
117-119 Clerkenwell Road
London, EC1R 5BY

Design & Art Direction
Julia
www.julia.uk.com

Publisher
Peter Huiberts
peter@frameweb.com

Sales & distribution
Benjamin Verheijden
benjamin@frameweb.com

Advertising
Germany:
Fadim Delice
fadim@frameweb.com

Switzerland:
Corinne Olejak
corinne@frameweb.com

USA:
Defne Aydintasbas
defne@frameweb.com

All other areas:
Peter Huiberts
peter@frameweb.com

Subscriptions
subscriptions@frameweb.com
www.frameweb.com

Subscription rates
EUR/CAN/USA
1-year €64.99
1-year student €54.99

How to subscribe?
Visit frameweb.com,
or call +31 20 4233 717

Elephant is published quarterly
by Frame Publishers BV
Laan der Hesperiden 68
1076 DX Amsterdam
The Netherlands
T +31 20 4233717
F +31 20 4280653
www.frameweb.com

ISSN 1879-3835
ISBN: 978-90-77174-56-2

Front cover
Ryan Gander, *An absolute
bereavement of the senses illustrated*
(Diptych detail), 2010
Photography credit: A. Burger

DISTRIBUTION

Australia
Speedimpex Australia
T +61 2 9698 4922
F +61 2 9698 7675
info@speedimpex.com.au

Austria
Morawa Pressevertrieb
T +43 1 5156 2190
F +43 1 5156 2881 955
mbaburek@morawa.com

Belgium
IMAPress
T +32 14 42 38 38
F +32 14 42 31 63
info@imapress.be

Belgium
Exhibitions International
T +32 16 296900
F +32 16 296129
info@exhibitionsinternational.be

Brazil
Freebook
T +55 11 3256 0577
F +32 11 3259 1120
informa@freebook.com.br

Canada
LMPI
T +1 514 355 5674
mcoutu@lmpi.com

Cyprus
Nasis
T +357 96 243125
niki@nasisbooks.com

Denmark
Interpress Danmark
T +45 3327 7744
F +45 3327 7701
ef@interpressdanmark.dk

Dubai
Tawseel Retail Distribution
T +971 4 344 2222
info@tawseel.com

Finland
Akateeminen Kirjakauppa
T +358 9 121 5910
F +358 9 121 4416
pasi.somari@stockmann.fi

France
Critiques Livres Distribution SAS
T +33 1 43 60 39 10
F +33 1 48 97 37 06
general@critiqueslivres.fr

Germany
IPS Pressevertrieb
T +49 2225 8801 182
F +49 2225 8801 59182
info@ips-d.de

Vice Versa Vertrieb
T +49 3061 6092 36
F +49 3061 6092 38
info@vice-versa-vertrieb.de

Greece
Papasotiriou Bookstores
T +30 10 3323 306
F +30 10 3848 254
diamantopoulos@papasotiriou.gr

Hong Kong
The Grand Commercial Co., Ltd.
T +852 2 570 9639
F +852 2 570 4665
thegrandcc@i-cable.com

Hungary
IPS Pressevertrieb
T +49 2225 8801 182
F +49 2225 8801 59182
lstulin@IPS-D.de

India
SBD Subscription Services
T +91 11 2871 4138
F +91 11 2871 2268
sbds@bol.net.in

Indonesia
Basheer Graphic Books
T +62 21 720 9151
F +62 21 720 9151
info@basheergraphic.com

Italy
Idea Books SRL
T +39 0445 576 574
F +39 0445 577 764
info@ideabooks.it

Japan
Memex
T +81 6 6281 2828
F +81 6 6258 4440
info@memex.ne.jp

DIP Inc.
T +81 3 5842 9053
info@dip-inc.co.jp

Middle East
AA Studio
T +961 1 990 199
F +961 1 990 188
aastudio@inco.com.lb

Malaysia
Basheer Graphic
T +60 2 713 2236
F +60 2 143 2236
info@basheergraphic.com

Netherlands
Betapress
T +31 161 457 800
F +31 161 453 161
m.maican@betapress.audax.nl

New Zealand
Mag Nation
T +64 9 3666216
info@magnation.com

Norway
Listo AB
T +46 8 792 46 68
carola.genas@listo.se

Portugal
International News Portugal
T +351 21 898 2010
mario.dias@internews.com.pt

Tema
T +351 21 342 4082
F +351 21 716 6925
belmiro@mail.telepac.pt

Poland
IPS Pressevertrieb
T +49 2225 8801 182
F +49 2225 8801 59182
lstulin@IPS-Pressevertrieb.de

Singapore
Basheer Graphic Books
T +65 336 0810
F +65 334 1950
info@basheergraphic.com

South Africa
Magscene
T +27 11 579 2000
F +27 11 579 2080
info@magscene.co.za

South Korea
TYM
T +82 2 390 8746
F +82 2 364 1341
eslee@tym.co.kr

Spain
Promotora de Prensa
Internacional SA
T +34 932 451 464
F +34 932 654 883
evelazquez@promopress.es

Sweden
Svenska Interpress AB
T +46 8 5065 0615
F +46 8 5065 0750
susanne.pettersson@interpress.se

Switzerland
IPS Pressevertrieb
T +49 2225 8801 182
F +49 2225 8801 59182
istulin@IPS-d.de

Thailand
Basheer Graphic Books
T +66 2391 9815
F +66 2391 9814
thai@basheergraphic.com

Taiwan
Long Sea
T +886 2 2706 6838
F +886 2 2706 6109
eric@longsea.com.tw

United Kingdom
COMAG
T+44 (0) 1895 433773
F+44 (0) 1895 433603
hazel.isaacs@comag.co.uk
andy.hounslow@comag.co.uk

Gestalten UK
T +44 20 7377 1388
F +44 20 7247 8624
l.williams@gestalten.com

United States
COMAG
T +44 20 1895 433733
F +44 20 1895 433603
louise.taylor@comag.co.uk

Consortium Book Sales
& Distribution
T +1 612 746-2600
F +1 612 746-2606
info@cbsd.com

Ubiquity Distributors Inc.
T 718-875-5491
F 718-875-8047
info@ubiquitymags.com

ELEPHANT (ISSN 1879-3835,
USPS No: 025-545)
is published quarterly :
Spring (April), Summer (July),
Autumn (October) & Winter
(January) by FRAME Publisher BV
and distributed in the US by DSW,
95 Aberdeen Road,
Emigsville PA 17318. Periodicals
postage paid at Emigsville, PA.
POSTMASTER: send address
changes to ELEPHANT,
PO Box 437,
EMIGSVILLE PA 17318-0437

Subscribe
to Elephant...

To subscribe and receive a free
copy of *Sketchbook*, please visit:

frameweb.com

Sketchbook is ideally suited for designers, graphic designers, illustrators, art directors and anyone working within creative industries. It's also a great resource for students and anyone interested in exploring his or her creativity.

The book was designed by Matt Willey and Zoe Bather of Studio8, an award-winning studio. They are obsessed with print and have designed – among many other print-based projects – books 100 Years of Menswear and Angaza Afrika, plus magazines Elephant, Futu, Map and Plastique.

Sketchbook

Illustrations
152 pages
240 x 180 mm
ISBN 9781856699044

MAGMA SKETCHBOOK

Design & Art Direction

Ideally suited for designers, graphic designers, illustrators, art directors and anyone working within the creative industries, or simply interested in exploring his or her creativity.

Sketchbooks for the Twenty-First Century

...and receive Sketchbook!

Rik Smits
7 Jan — 11 Feb

Pencil drawings
Galerie Ron Mandos, Amsterdam
www.ronmandos.nl

Born: The Hague, Netherlands, 1982
Medium: Drawing
Key Themes & Ideas: These landscapes of an imaginary city work as a metaphor for our modern society, exploring the relationship between religion and capitalism. The ambition towards power and status has made capitalism the main ideology of its inhabitants and become a religion in itself. The emptiness of these deserted cities embodies the lost moral standards and values of humanity.

Hemsley Park, 2011, pencil on paper, 50 x 70 cm

The 32 Penn Avenue State Monument, 2001, pencil on paper, 21 x 29 cm

The IC Center by Night, 2010, pencil on paper, 21 x 29 cm

Ingres Turkish Bath (Chicks with Dicks), 2008, charcoal on paper, 140 x 140 cm

Trevor Guthrie
Now — 21 Jan

Trevor Guthrie
Barbarian Art Gallery, Zurich
www.barbarian-art.com

Born: Dunfermile, Scotland, 1964
Residence: Zurich, Switzerland
Medium: Drawing
Key Themes & ideas: According to the artist, his favourite themes are: 'American foreign policy, the medieval debate between science and religion and art history – in that particular order'. After working mainly from Polaroid photographs for fifteen years, Guthrie has started using found imagery in order to create large charcoal drawings. Realistic, gloomy, his work is often a reflection of his dark humour.
Quote: 'I think a political climate anywhere, good or bad, is material for an artist – he should only be free to express himself.'

galerie bob van orsouw

albisriederstrasse 199a   ch-8047 zurich
phone +41 (0)44 273 11 00
mail@bobvanorsouw.ch   www.bobvanorsouw.ch

haluk akakçe
philip akkerman
nobuyoshi araki
armen eloyan
hannah greely
anton henning

november 19, 2011
until
february 4, 2012

philip akkerman
albrecht schnider

teresa hubbard/
alexander birchler
peter kamm
edward lipski
lutz & guggisberg

february 11, 2012
until
april 14, 2012

the gallery collection
exhibition curated by beda achermann

daido moriyama
paul morrison
ernesto neto
julian opie
walter pfeiffer
david reed

february 3–8, 2012

vip art fair, exclusively online

albrecht schnider
shirana shahbazi
hannah van bart
marcel van eeden
bernard voïta
mario ybarra jr.

march 8–11, 2012

the armory show, new york

Graphic Design: Now in Production
Now—22 Jan

Graphic Design: Now in Production
Walker Art Centre, Target and Friedman Galleries, Minneapolis
www.walkerart.org

Brief: Graphic design has broadened its reach and appeal dramatically over the past decade and is continuing to do so, expanding from a specialized profession to a widely deployed tool. This everything-included exhibition explores some of most dominant and exciting sectors and genres of graphic design, including posters, books, magazines, identity and branding, information graphics, typography and film title graphics.

Forever, 2003, 42 bicycles, 275 x 450 cm, photography by Ai Weiwei

Julião Sarmento
7 Jan — 18 Feb

Julião Sarmento
Galerie Daniel Templon, Paris
www.danieltemplon.com

Ai Weiwei
18 Nov — 12 Feb

Ai Weiwei
Louisiana, Copenhagen
www.louisiana.dk

Born: Lisbon, Portugal, 1948
Residence: Estoril, Portugal
Media: Film, video, painting, sculpture, installation, multimedia
Key Themes & Ideas: Explores desire and its representation through collages of photography, graphite drawings and words.
Quote: 'The subject is that which is not there.'

Media: Film and installation
Debt Allegedly Owed the Chinese Government: $2.3 million
Description of Pieces in Exhibition: Forever, a cyclical tower of bicycles which, without handles or pedals, can go nowhere; *Fountain of Light*, a crystal tower that will be placed in the garden; *Trees*, a sculpture made out of trunks and branches as a metaphor of growth and life.
Quote: 'Without freedom of speech there is no modern world, just a barbaric one.'
Incidental Fact: The artist is regarded as a top professional blackjack player in gambling circles.

Rosson Crow
25 Feb — 31 Mar

Rosson Crow
Honor Fraser, Los Angeles
www.honorfraser.com

Born: Dallas, USA, 1982
Residence: Los Angeles, USA
Medium: Painting
Description: We enter the hall of what looks like an old theatre with two staircases going up, one on the left, one on the right, to then meet, somewhere the middle. There are various openings, but none of them is quite a door. The paint on the walls looks faded; the pictures have blood red backgrounds. The whole image seems to be melting, even down to the red and gold pattern on the carpet. From afar, the whole looks a face in a helmet, or a skull staring back at us.
Adjectives: theatrical, immersive, fluttering, decadent

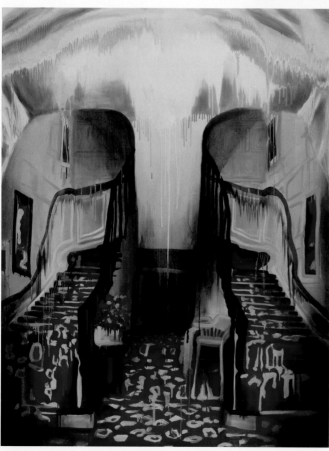

Stairway at Rosalie Plantation, 2011, acrylic and oil on canvas, 274.3 x 213.7 cm

Untitled (Dust Bowl), 2011, acrylic and oil on canvas, 213.7 x 274.3 cm

Subscribe and Save

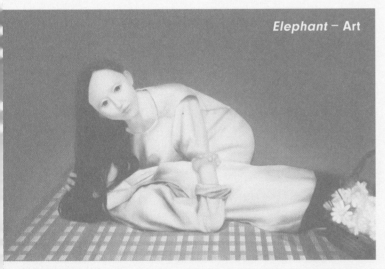

Subscription Form

Choose Subscription

Frame

☐ **1 year** 6 issues	**€95**
☐ **1 year student*** 6 issues	**€75**
☐ **2 year** 12 issues	**€180**
☐ **2 year student*** 12 issues	**€140**

Mark

☐ **1 year** 6 issues	**€95**
☐ **1 year student*** 6 issues	**€75**
☐ **2 year** 12 issues	**€180**
☐ **2 year student*** 12 issues	**€140**

Elephant

☐ **1 year** 4 issues	**€65**
☐ **1 year student*** 4 issues	**€55**
☐ **2 year** 8 issues	**€120**
☐ **2 year student*** 8 issues	**€100**

Rates include VAT and shipping costs.
Subscription starts after receipt of payment.

* Students: Please enclose a copy of your student registration form.

10% discount on any additional subscriptions

Return this form via

Email shop@frameweb.com
Fax +31 20 4280 653
Or post to
Frame Publishers
Attn. Subscriptions Department
Laan der Hesperiden 68
1076 DX Amsterdam
The Netherlands

Delivery Address

Name

Company

Address

Post code   City

Country

Phone

Email

Payment

☐ **Please send me an invoice**
☐ **Please charge my credit card:**

  ☐ Visa
  ☐ MasterCard
  ☐ American Express

Credit card number

Expiry date ☐ ☐ / ☐ ☐ (mm/yy)
CVC2 code   ☐ ☐ ☐

(Last 3 digits on the back of your card.
For Amex: 4 digits printed on the front of your card.)

Name of card holder

Signature

Hans van Bentem

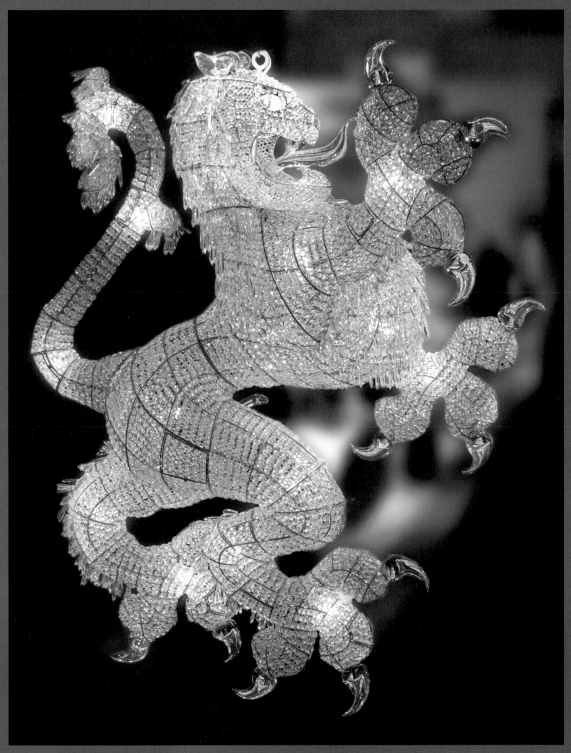

LION
Bohemian crystal chandelier, 2006, unique.

CLAUDIA KAPP
25.11.2011 – 29.1.2012

YOU YOU

EDITH-RUSS-HAUS for Media Art
Katharinenstraße 23
D-26121 Oldenburg

Opening Hours:
Tuesday – Friday 2.00 – 6.00 p.m.
Saturday and Sunday 11.00 a.m. – 18.00 p.m.
Monday closed

www.edith-russ-haus.de

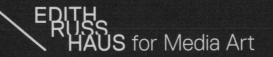

 STADT OLDENBURG i.O.

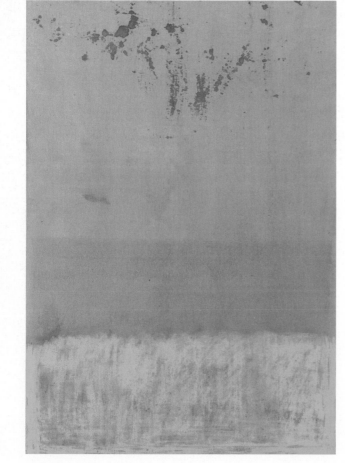

Untitled, 2011, acrylic and pastel on linen, 183 x 127 cm

Sergej Jensen
12 Jan — 18 Feb

Sergej Jensen
Anton Kern Gallery, New York
www.antonkerngallery.com

Born: Maglegaard, Denmark, 1973
Residence: Berlin, Germany
Medium: Painting
Key Themes & ideas: Jensen centres his work around the physical act of creating. He paints, sews, bleaches or stains the canvases. He is a manipulator, a recycler and an 'assemblagist'. Particularly interest in materials, he incorporates a variety of fabrics into his work. The result are tactile, subtle forms and colours, doing their work somewhere between abstraction and representation.

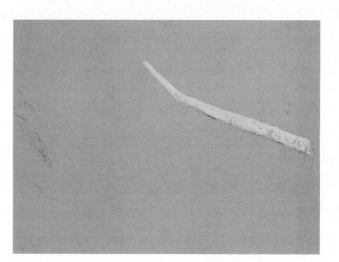

Untitled, 2011, oil and glass beads on linen, 132 x 183 cm

On Kawara
6 Jan — 11 Feb

Date Painting(s) in New York & 136 Other Cities
David Zwirner, New York
www.davidzwirner.com

MAR. 30, 2001, 2001, from 'Today' series, 1966- 'Friday', Acrylic on canvas, 25.4 x 33 cm

Born: Kariya, Japan, 1933
Residence: New York, intermittent
Medium: Conceptual painting
Key Themes & ideas: Time, and its duration, though it might appear to be objective through the standardized systems we have created to measure it, is always ultimately a subjective experience understood in and through the present moment.
Today Series: On Kawara has been since 1966 working on this series. They consist of monochromatic paintings, in one of eight predetermined sizes, horizontal, the white type indicating the date when the painting was executed (always in one day). On Kawara has worked in more than 112 cities around the world.

Untitled, 2010, Unique, Two digital C-prints, Mount: Plexiglas, sintra 52.1 x 84.8cm and 78.1 x 84.8 cm, Installed dimensions: 78.1 x 182.4 x 12.7 cm

Marlo Pascual
16 Feb — 24 Mar

Marlo Pascual
Casey Kaplan, New York
www.caseykaplangallery.com

Untitled, 2011, Unique, Digital C-Print, rock
Print size: 135.9 x 152.4 cm

Born: Nashville, USA, 1972
Residence: New York, USA
Medium: Installation
Key Themes & ideas: Using found imagery and genre photographs – head shots, still lives, nudes, pin-ups – as a starting point for her work, Marlo Pascual plays with images, cropping and enlarging them, displaying them with found objects, injecting new life and meaning into their subjects. By breaking the picture plane for which the photographs were initially created, she creates a new logic, leaving behind their representational intrinsic value and turning them in 3-dimensional sculptures.

Sanya Kantarovsky
18 Feb — 24 Mar

Sanya Kantarovsky
Marc Foxx, Los Angeles
www.marcfoxx.com

Born: Moscow, Russia, 1982
Residence: Los Angeles, USA
Media: Painting and sculpture
Subject: A thin figure, most likely female, stands under a shower; body loose, head bent, hair hanging down, one arm dangling while the other holds the back of her head. The figure gives out the feeling of letting of one's muscular tension go and retreating into oneself under the pouring warm water. The floor is light blue, possibly wet and vaguely reflective. Water appears to be moving, accumulating into limpid pools of blue watercolour on the edges of the canvas. Light shines from a rectangle representing what could be a glass door and the outside world.
Quote: 'There is a sign for everything: author's block, emptiness, loneliness, awe, dilemma... It gets interesting when this vocabulary is framed through a more hermetic language.'
A Few Adjectives: hermetic, expressive, tactile, geometric, ordinary, extraordinary.

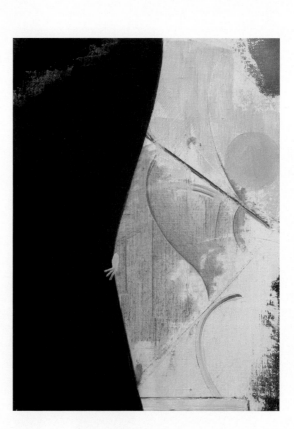

Untitled, 2011, Powder coated steel, two oil on linen paintings.
Each panel, includes 2 paintings 86.4 x 66 cm. Each: 203.2 x 116.84 x 2.54 cm

Untitled, 2011, Gesso, oil and watercolor. 30.5 x 40.6 cm

ARTWORKS ARE LIKE FRIENDSHIPS.
THEY CONNECT BEYOND ALL BORDERS.
THEY INSPIRE AND OFTEN PROVOKE
THE UNEXPECTED.

AB GALLERY promotes contemporary Islamic Art and represents artists mainly from the Middle East and Iran.

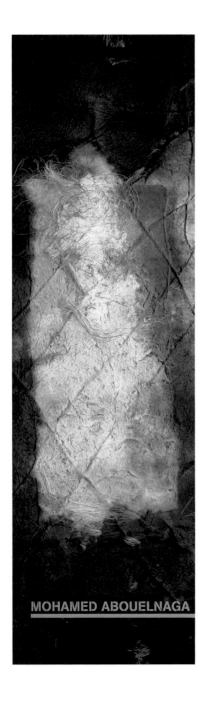

MOHAMED ABOUELNAGA

HALIM AL KARIM

AB GALLERY LUCERNE

Arealstrasse 6
CH-6020 Emmenbrücke-
Lucerne

Phone +41 41 982 08 80
Mobil   +41 79 69 805 69
E-mail office@ab-gallery.com

**AB GALLERY ZURICH +
AB PROJECTS**

Klausstrasse 23
CH-8008 Zurich

Phone +41 41 982 08 80
Mobil   +41 79 69 805 69
E-mail office@ab-gallery.com

AB GALLERY Switzerland
www.ab-gallery.com

AB GALLERY
across borders

Veron Urdarianu
3 Mar — 14 Apr

Veron Urdarianu
Galerie Zink, Berlin
www.galeriezink.de

Born: Bucharest, Romania, 1951
Residence: Amsterdam, Netherlands
Medium: Oil painting
Description: Originally trained as a sculptor, Urdarianu works his canvases maintaining a three dimensionality of layers, leaving behind the scotch tape that artists use to create clear edges, collaging shapes of cardboard and paper, and ultimately tying together the pieces with a layer of paint. The nostalgic feel comes through the use of subtle colours and muted tones. Different perspectives are used in the same painting like fragments of an object, fitting into one another like the parts of a puzzle or the shards of a broken glass pane.

Graduated, 2007/2010, oil and tape on canvas, 60 x 50 cm

El Salvador, 2010, oil and tape on canvas, 50 x 60 cm

Steff Loewenbaum
17 Feb — 14 Mar

Random Exhibition Generator
Artary Gallery, Stuttgart
www.artary.de

Born: Stuttgart, Germany, 1975
Residence: Stuttgart, Berlin
Medium: mixed media and sculpture
Beginnings: Ten years as a DJ from the age of eighteen. Founded the first temporary electronic music club in Stuttgart, where his artistic career took off – first through creating promotional flyers for the club, and then through curating his own shows in a club-owned gallery space. He co-founded art society Dialekt e.V. Kunstverein, organizing international art shows in vacant spaces in the city.
Key Themes & Ideas: The creation of the individual self as an opposition between society and reality. Dark desires, guilt, victimhood, voyeurism, passiveness and lust for violence. The self-generated demons of the subconscious.

DAZED & CONFUSED
Magazine
Now — 29 Jan

20 Years of Dazed & Confused Magazine, Making It Up As We Go Along exhibition
Somerset House, London
www.somersethouse.org.uk

Notes: Coinciding with the release of the book of the same name the exhibition will chart the 20 strong years of Dazed & Confused magazines history. Launched in London in 1991 by Jefferson Hack and photographer Rankin it quickly drew a strong coveted following and became a creative platform for musicians and artists alike. Work featured in the exhibition includes groundbreaking photography by Rankin, Nick Knight, David Sims and Terry Richardson alongside specially commissioned projects by Jake & Dinos Chapman, Damien Hirst and Sam Taylor-Wood with selected designs from British fashion powerhouses Alexander McQueen, Vivienne Westwood and Gareth Pugh.

Page 15 – *Kate Moss,* June 1998, Photography by Rankin, styling by Katie Grand

David Lieske
19 Jan — 25 Feb

Style and Subversion 1979 - 2012
Corvi-Mora, London
www.corvi-mora.com

Untitled (Reading Septem Sermones Ad Mortuos), 2006, Bromine Silver Gelantine Print on Ilford Multigrade FB 5K. 179 x 122 cm (framed), Edition: 2 + I AP. Courtesy: Corvi-Mora, London

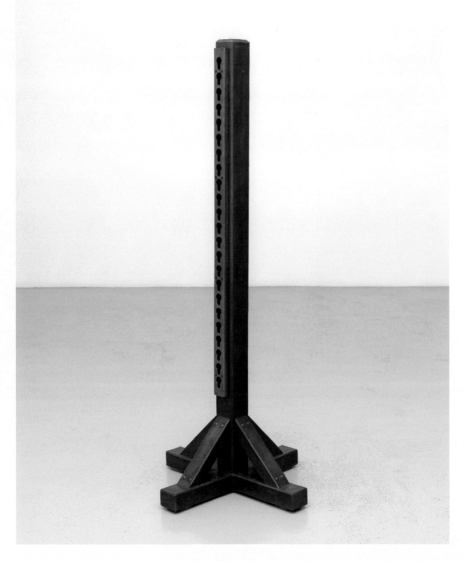

Form IX (Case Arse), 2008, bronze, 158 x 50 x 50 cm

Born: Hamburg, Germany, 1979
Residence: Berlin, Germany
Medium: Installation, collage
Key Themes & ideas: The dichotomy between the public person and the real self. What it means to be an artist and the idealization of the aura of the artist.
Quote: 'You might want to ask me now why it is that I want to be an artist and I can only answer that there is probably not any other professional field (besides perhaps organized crime, which I happen to feel drawn to) that would tolerate an existence like mine. Which, for me, is reason enough to insist on being an artist.'

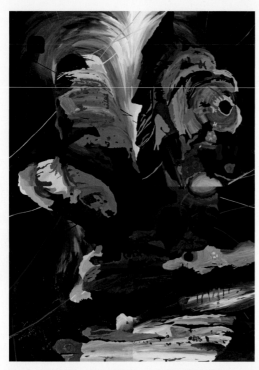

Hopes Noes, 2011, enamel and oil on aluminum, 600 x 500 cm, courtesy the artist and Stuart shave Modern Art, London

Clare Woods
Now — 29 Jan

Clare Woods: The Unquiet Head
The Hepworth Wakefield, Yorkshire
www.hepworthwakefield.org

Brief: The British painter graduated from Goldsmiths College in 1999 and has exhibited internationally. Her paintings are often visually ambiguous, even somewhat claustrophobic, yet completely engaging, with their lush use of paint. Her current works explore the power and history of rock formations in reference to the British landscape.

The Intended, 2011, Enamel & oil on aluminium,

Gary Hume
18 Jan — 18 Feb

The Indifferent Owl
White Cube Mason's Yard
and Hoxton Square, London
www.whitecube.com

Plaits 3, 2011, Gloss paint on aluminium

Born: Tenterden, UK, 1962
Medium: Gloss paint on aluminium
Description: his work, though rather uncharacteristic, is still strongly identified with the YBA's of the 1990's. He has, however, more than any other artist of his generation, been conducting an intense dialogue with the British painting tradition, from Turner and Bacon to Auerbach and Caufield – with Julian Opie and Michael Craig Martin on the sofa and his works echoing on a space, a colourful limbo, all their own.
Quote: 'Art is not about absolute concrete affirmations. Art has questions and doubts and ups and downs of preference.'

DESIGN IN BOIJMANS

Design in Boijmans

New Energy in Design and Art
29.10.2011 - 26.02.2012

Intervention #18
Sheila Hicks - Cent Minimes
26.11.2011 - 04.03.2012

Rotterdam Design Prize 2011
26.11.2011 - 12.02.2012

Museum Boijmans Van Beuningen is the Dutch podium for national and international design talent. This autumn, the programme 'Design in Boijmans' features a series of special exhibitions: a group show focussing on design proposals for a sustainable world, a survey of the nominees for the prestigious Rotterdam Design Prize 2011, and a presentation of the work of artist Sheila Hicks. In 2012 the museum is presenting its new displays of the collection of design and a series of presentations of the newest developments in design.

www.boijmans.nl

with the kind support of:

Eneco   BankGiroLoterij   Ploum Lodder Princen
advocaten notarissen

museum van
boijmans beuningen

Dunne & Raby, Technological Dreams Series: No. 1, Robots, 2007, photo: Per Tingleff

Santiago Sierra
31 Jan — 31 Mar

Santiago Sierra
Lisson Gallery, London
www.lissongallery.com

Born: Madrid, Spain, 1966
Residence: Mexico City, Mexico
Medium: Video
Key Themes & Ideas: Politically charged and highly controversial, his work became widely known through his practice of hiring unprivileged people to accomplish degrading actions. This points at the hidden structures of power at work in our economy: exploiting the marginalized and disenfranchised through the allure of work. A new exhibition presents his recent work, NO, GLOBAL TOUR, which documents the journey of a big sculpture (NO), a big 3-D 'NO' affirming the assertive power of humanity.
Quote: 'We are all, absolutely all, submitted to the reproduction and the circulation of the capital. [...] Persons are objects of the State and of Capital and are employed as such.'

Unita di Pressione - Le Tenebre, 2011, oil on linen, 300 x 196 cm
Courtesy Dennis Kimmerich, New York; greengrassi, London

NO GLOBAL TOUR I, From the Carpenter shop to the former stable, Lucca, Italy, July 2009, Courtesy the artist and Lisson Gallery

Margherita Manzelli
19 Jan — 25 Feb

Margherita Manzelli
Greengrassi, London
www.greengrassi.com

Born: Ravena, Italy, 1968
Residence: Milan, Italy
Medium: Oil on canvas
Description: Manzelli's work is strangely captivating. She depicts ethereal and imaginary female figures. Portrayed in strained postures and abstract backgrounds, her characters look abandoned. Their direct gaze creates an unsettling empathy with the viewer, inviting us to join them in the suspension of time and space which they inhabit.
Quote: 'I would like them to be different to me. And yet I realize that this very desire is symptomatic of the fact that something of myself remains in them.'

World of inspiration

Don't forget to put these dates in your diary: from the 25th to the 27th of January 2012 Material Xperience takes place. This year the inspiring event for creative professionals and manufacturers is centred around the exciting opportunities that internationalisation presents to designers and architects. For free entrance please register at www.materialxperience.com.

25 to 27 January 2012, Ahoy Rotterdam, The Netherlands

Material Xperience

January 25—27, 2012   m a t = r i a

———— **Dutch edition** ————

Material Xperience is organised by

m a t = r i a   **architectenweb**   **GEVEL** 2012   ▼ **vnu** exhibitions europe

Sponsored by

Anything is possible™

Boris Savelev
2 Dec — 21 Jan

Colour Constructions
Michael Hoppen Gallery, London
www.michaelhoppengallery.com

Sun Basket, © Boris Savelev, Multi-layered pigment print on gesso coated aluminium 164.2 x 109.4 cm. Courtesy of Michael Hoppen Gallery

Garage, © Boris Savelev, Multi-layered pigment print on gesso coated aluminium 164.2 x 109.4 cm. Courtesy of Michael Hoppen Gallery

Born: Chernowitz, Ukraine, 1948
Residence: Moscow, Russia
Bio: Graduated in 1972 from the Aviation Institute in Moscow. Savelev worked as an aeronautical engineer, while cultivating photography as a hobby. Completely self-taught, he started working as a freelance photographer concomitantly to his professional career. It was in 1983 that he devoted himself completely to his photographic and artistic path.
Medium: Photography
Key Themes & Ideas: His personal use of the photographic tools and procedures transforms the ordinary everyday moments and objects into extraordinary, mysterious epiphanies. Although once defined by the Guardian as 'elegant observational realism', his style is far from documentary and creates seemingly non-representational and emotionally charged images.
Notable Fact: Savelev's pictures are printed onto gesso coated aluminium panels at Factum Arte in Madrid with a custom-made flatbed multilayer pigment printer. The richly tonal effect is refined by hand and further enhanced by waxing.

No Fashion, Please!
Now — 22 Jan

No Fashion, Please!
Kunsthalle Wien, Vienna
www.kunsthallewien.at

Viviane Sassen, HKAOI, 2006, © Viviane Sassen, Courtesy Viviane Sassen

Subject: No Fashion, Please! – an exhibition addressing the relationship between body, clothing and fashion photography, focusing on the changing aesthetics of the body (and ideals related to it) in the last two decades.
On the red carpet: Chan-Hyo Bae, Tracey Baran, Jeff Bark, Leigh Bowery/Fergus Greer, Steven Cohen/Marianne Greber, Philip-Lorca diCorcia, Matthias Herrmann, Lea Golda Holterman, Izima Kaoru, Luigi & Luca, Sandra Mann, Martin & The evil eyes of Nur, Brigitte Niedermair, Erwin Olaf, Alex Prager, Hanna Putz, Viviane Sassen, Sophia Wallace, Bruce Weber

Sandra Mann, 23|100-0002 Sandra with Beard, 2000, © Sandra Mann und/and VBK Wien, 2011 Courtesy Sandra Mann

Marko Maettam
2 Feb — 11 Mar

Marko Maettam solo show
Nettie Horn Gallery, London
www.nettiehorn.com

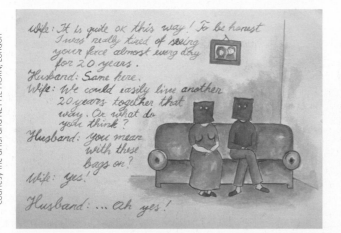

30 Stories (detail), 2010. Series of 30 drawings Pen and watercolour on paper, 21 x 29.7 cm Courtesy the artist and NETTIE HORN, London

Born: Viljandi, Estonia, 1965
Residence: Tallin, Estonia
Medium: Sculpture, video animation, photography, drawing
Key Themes & Ideas: For his first solo show in the UK, Marko Maettam presents a varied range of works linked together by a subtle reflection on family life and the varied emotional states that its normal routine can trigger. With irreverent irony and at times apparently immature naughtiness, he transforms everyday moments into ferocious sketches. All of this visual universe is 'seasoned' with a therapeutic playfulness.

Industry
of Nature

Another
Approach
to Ecology

A beautifully illustrated book on mimicking nature to create sustainable designs

frameweb.com

FRAM3

Jānis Avotiņš
Jan — Feb

Jānis Avotiņš
Ibid Projects, London
www.ibidprojects.com

Foreign, 2011, oil on canvas, 47,4 x 52,8 cm

Born: Riga, Latvia, 1981
Medium: Painting
Key Themes & Ideas: Translation of historical photographs from the Soviet era into painting. Elimination of the original contextual background, the remaining portraits becoming abstracted from any historical narrative, hovering in an almost monochrome, neutral and silent atmosphere. The overall sens of visual fading questions the actuality of the archetypes in the Soviet collective memory.

Tension, 2011, oil on canvas, 49,8 x 87,6 cm

Jerzy Treutler
2 Feb — 17 Mar

Mr T: The Posters Of Jerzy Treutler, Solo Show
Kemistry Gallery, London
www.kemistrygallery.co.uk

Medium: Graphic design
Brief: Born in 1931 and having created over one hundred posters, several book covers and a range of logos, Jerzy Treutler can only be described as a design veteran. He is internationally recognized for his collaboration with the school of Polish poster design, working for films, exhibitions, sport and national information. The exhibition, Treutler's first UK solo show, serves to demonstrate his skill in defining a brand. Treutler's bold style and use of abstract design, typical of the Polish poster artist, underline the strength of a message.

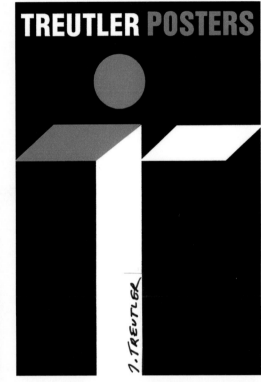

V ogne broda net (1967), poster 1970, 58.5 x 84 cm, offset

with The Polish Ministry of Culture, B1, Offset Print

Five Easy Pieces (1970)/ film poster (1974), A1, offset print, CWF- Central Film Agency. dir. Bob Rafelson

Exhibition Poster, Jerzy Treutler (2011) A1, Offset Print

Books to be put under the Christmas Tree, Publishers House Dom Ksiazki

PAPER SCISSOR STONE
STORE

GUP

INTERNATIONALLY RENOWNED
PHOTOGRAPHY MAGAZINE
WWW.GUPMAGAZINE.COM

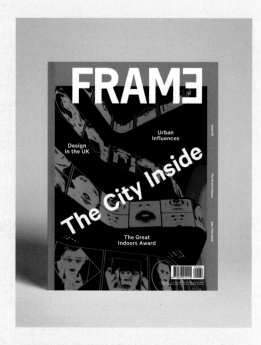

Artists:

.: Reto Camenisch
.: Corinne Güdemann
.: Dieter Hall
.: Peter Kröning
.: Urs Marty
.: Andrea Muheim
.: Thomas Ott
.: Karoline Schreiber
.: Hans Witschi

Current & Upcoming Exhibitions:

December 9th – February 10th
Robert Honegger: Honegger's World - Paintings and Kinetic Objects

March 2nd – March 28th
Andrea Bischof & Hermann Kremsmayer: Two Painters from Vienna

Outside exhibitions:

Andrea Muheim: Moods – Paintings
December 10th – February 10th
Suvretta House, St. Moritz

Peter Kröning: Sculptures in Wood
December 20th – April 15th
Andrea Robbi Museum, Sils Maria

Galerie & Edition Stephan Witschi
Zwinglistrasse 12
CH-8004 Zurich
0041 44 242 37 27
0041 44 242 37 28 (fax)
edition@stephanwitschi.ch
www.stephanwitschi.ch

Open Wednesday to Friday 14h – 18h,
Saturday 13h – 17h, or by appointment

**GALERIE & EDITION
STEPHAN WITSCHI**

Anna Bjerger

A LONG GLIMPSE

Born: 1973, Skallsjo, Sweden.

Trained: Central St Martins and Royal College of Art, London.

Lives: Småland, Sweden.

In broad strokes: Anna Bjerger's pictures are painted from photographs rather than life, their subjects derived from out-of-date reference books, instruction manuals, gardening books and magazines. Familiar, anonymous, intimate, yet curiously disconnected, these are unsettling narratives; the meanings becoming slippery and ambiguous. The pictures also call attention to the physicality of their medium. Paint is applied wet-on-wet in broad brushstrokes over aluminium panels. The speed with which the works have been painted seems to strive after the instantaneous quality of photography, while at the same time asserting the transformative nature of painting.

Influences and inspiration: 'For as long as I can remember, I have wanted to be an artist in a romantic sense. I was nineteen and went to Germany with my lithography course to look at art, and I was confronted with German Expressionism, George Baselitz and also Marlene Dumas. And there are so many other artists... Edward Munch, Vincent Van Gogh, Vija Celmins, Otto Dix, August Renoir, Robert Ryman, Hanna Wilkes – the list is long. When at a loss, I turn to Philip Guston's writing and paintings.'

References: 'I mainly use found imagery, occasionally a personal photo will find its way into the studio. The process of collecting photographic material, looking through images, finding arbitrary connections and making a selection of what to paint is a big part of my work. Photographs contain ambiguity and are instantaneous objects of the past – to me they are a great inspiration. If I were thinking in terms of painting "live", I would find it daunting to consider the boundaries of the space I am depicting.'

Process: 'I think of this process – painting a photo – as a way of deciphering an image. I want it to be an intuitive and almost subconscious act, which is why I like to start a painting in the morning, first thing when I get into the studio. I don't think of it as an original, or a copy – the painting is a hybrid. When I paint the photograph, I don't change the composition or the framing, but I might exaggerate certain areas.'

Workplace: 'My studio is in an old school situated in the forest in the south of Sweden. It is a red wooden building from the turn of the last century; the only source of heating is a log fire. My husband, who is also painter, shares the space with me. We live in the school teacher's house next door.'

Painting: 'Painting should get under your skin. It is a balancing act between control and the accidental. Painting is the subject of my work: everything around it is just a way of making sense of it.'

Brushwork: 'I am using the paint and the brush marks to clarify the depicted image. I hope the painting exudes confidence, meaning it could be executed no other way. The texture of oil paint, colour, light and surface – it never ceases to engage me.'

Speed: 'I make a painting in one session; if it doesn't work I reject it. I keep the source material around the studio for a while before painting, so that it becomes familiar. To be able to capture a certain mood I have to keep the pace up not to lose momentum when painting.'

Rhythm: 'I tend to have months in which I paint every day, when I am in a flow. These periods are followed by months when I am not making much work, but spend my time thinking, reading and collecting visual material.'

www.gabrielrolt.com
www.davidrisleygallery.com

Man with light, 2011, oil on aluminum panel, 90 x 75 cm, Photo: Peter Tijhuis
Courtesy of Anna Bjerger and Galerie Gabriel Rolt, Amsterdam

Repose, 2011, oil on aluminum panel, 120 x 60 cm, Photo: Peter Tijhuis
Courtesy of Anna Bjerger and Galerie Gabriel Rolt, Amsterdam

Smile, 2010, oil on aluminium panel, 30x40cm
Courtesy of Anna Bjerger and Galerie Gabriel Rolt, Amsterdam

Shoot, 2010, oil on aluminium panel, 80x70 cm
Courtesy of Anna Bjerger and Galerie Gabriel Rolt, Amsterdam

Hell'O Monsters

SIX-HANDED

By Ana Ibarra

Hell'O Monsters exhibit in galleries and museums, working with graffiti, drawing and collage – three minds working together; drawing with six hands to tell stories of a dreamlike world full of strange creatures.

— *Who is Hell'O Monsters?* Hell'O is an artist collective based in Brussels, Belgium. It's formed by three people: Jérôme Meynen, Antoine Detaille and François Dieltiens. Most of the time we work with six hands over the same drawing with, let's say, a similar style to create a kind of natural unity.

— *How did you meet?* We met ten years ago over [graffiti] walls. We became friends and created the first collective because there was an affinity of styles and also ideas. After a few years together we decided to create Hell'O because our work started to take shape. Just walls and friendly artistic actions started to feel like not enough, and we felt the desire – and found the energy – to create something specific.

— *How did you come up with the name 'Hell'o Monsters'?* There are several reasons. First for the polarity of the word: between hello and hell. On the one hand it has a positive connotation of saying 'welcome', but, in contrast, it can be seen as an invitation to a darker side. We believe that in fact this polarity is very present in our work, where nothing is really good or bad and where 'ambiguity' is a major notion. 'Monsters' is used for the symbolic representation of the human evil side. Although we don't know exactly where it comes from, we seem to be obsessed by this negativity.

— *What is the inspiration behind your work?* Inspiration comes from the different aspects of human nature: goodness and evil, hope and failure, and other dichotomies and terms in between. Those signs give us access to a rich world, full of energy. Of course there's lots of personal worries and feelings. We try to use the tools of mythology and philosophy, translating all those things into metaphoric or allegoric representations.

— *How does the creative process work?* It took us a long time to have a coherent base and a proper process to work together. Now it has become really natural to draw together everyday. Normally we compose the basic structure in advance; the technique and the colours, if any, and after, we draw freely without thinking too much about it and slowly create a dynamic world between the different ideas.

— *Do you share a studio?* We share a studio in a building with other artists, which gives us the opportunity to work in a regular way. It is in the centre of Brussels, just a few metres away from the 'Bourse'. Our studio has become a kind of meeting point – a space where our friends and other artists are always welcome, so there are always things happening. It's full of nice moments.

— *Do you divide the tasks?* We have not established specific roles, and it doesn't seem to matter, but each of us has his or her own little trends. Anybody can decide what he wants to do. For us it's more about the energy. We all try to do our best.

— *How would you describe your art? Street art, graphic design, illustration?* The first exhibition we did was in a little gallery in Brussels. At the time we were working a lot on walls and much less on paper, but the gallerist had seen our work through the internet and wanted us to show in his space. After that our work has been more focused on paper and installations and less on walls. After a few projects and exhibitions, our convictions and intentions grew clearer and stronger. But being objective, I'd say that most of our work is on paper and really figurative, so it's illustration. But we also work on installation, video and sculpture, although we almost never work for commercial requests. Our work is exhibited in galleries, museums or art centres. I don't know if this helps to classify the work that we do. Anyway, frontiers and labels seem a bit stupid to us.

— *What are the advantages of each medium?* At the moment we are very attached to black and white drawing on paper, because we think it is a really clear technique and gives a darker atmosphere to our drawings. But when you use the same technique for a while, you can get tired and start feeling trapped. The absence of colour gives a superficial or aesthetic aspect of similarity, but it also becomes less fun as a process, more repetitive.

— *Do you think street art is gaining a better reputation nowadays?* Street art... Architecture is on the street and is not called street art. I don't feel very comfortable with this label, it is just an invention, sorry. I mean there is art in the street, there is vandalism, and there are shitty and good things everywhere. Indoors it becomes art. There is urban installation, public art. It is just market vocabulary. I just want to draw, I always wanted to. If somebody wants to give me money for the hours I spend doing it and keep the drawing and enjoy watching it, perfect, I will continue making this.

— *Any future plans?* To work – because it works! We expect to continue together, doing things all around the world, and to travel, and get better, and learn new things, and have kids, stop wars, buy a dog and a car, and be happy...

hellomonsters.wordpress.com
www.jas-gallery.com

Rendlesham Forest, 1980, 2007, graphite, digital, 50.8 x 33.02 cm
for Crafty Magazine

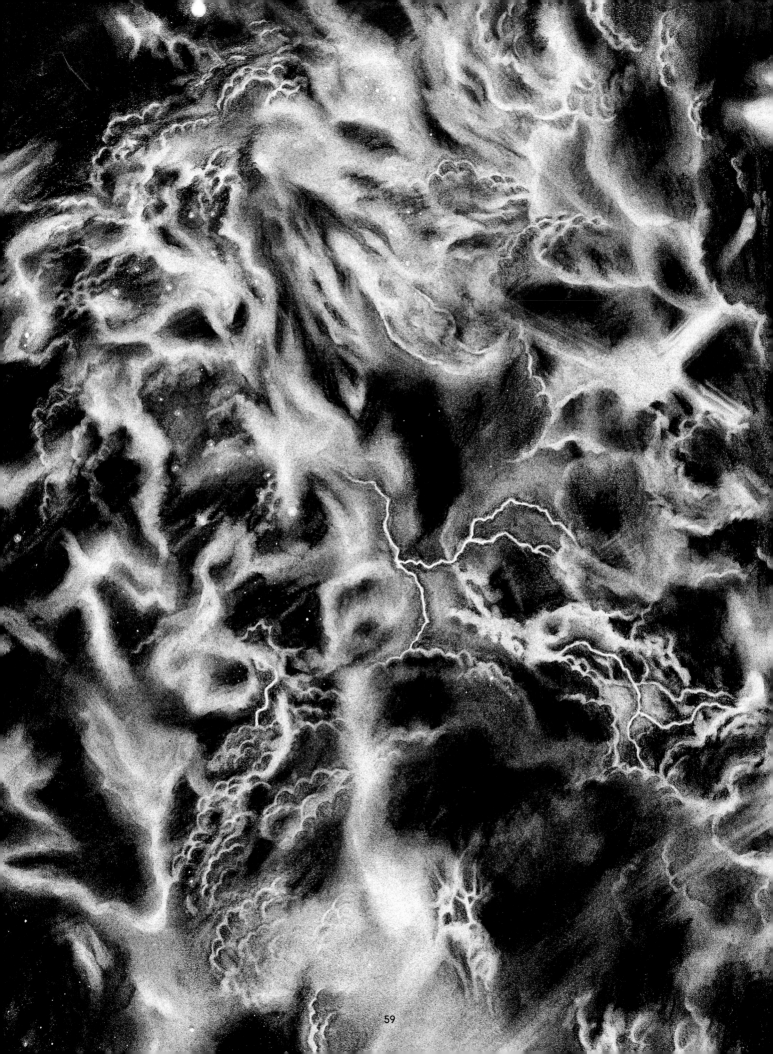

There's a name for this movement: 'transitionists'. So I guess if I was to consider myself a part of a community at all, it would be that one

Untitled (There Ol), Photo collage

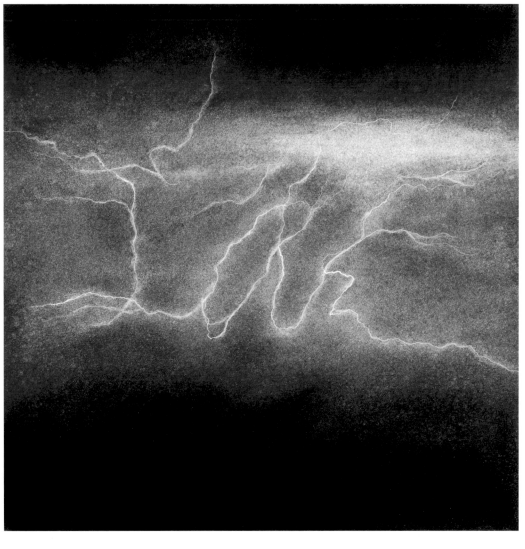

Love, charcoal on paper

Ruggero Maramotti

A VISUAL JOURNAL

by Margherita Dessanay

The work of Italian photographer Ruggero Maramotti is recognizable for his personal and delicate use of light. His avoidance of high saturations gives his pictures a soft quality, like the ancient 'flavour' a dusty patina gives silver pieces in an antiques shop. Maramotti's images linger in an atmosphere between old-fashioned and timeless. He says his most recurrent subjects are 'empty landscapes, flora and intimate places'. There may be an implicit connection with his childhood, a 'nice prison' in his own words. While he was growing up in Parma, Maramotti's family used to live in the suburbs close to a fast road. 'Because of that road I was forced to spend my childhood playing in the garden or in the fields beside my house.' Ruggero left Parma when he was twenty-three. After a period spent between Milan and Paris, first as a photo-assistant and later as a photographer in the fashion industry, in 2004 he went on holiday to Stockholm: 'There I had a sort of epiphany: I realized I didn't like the Italian aggressive attitude. It was a pleasure to run away and re-discover nature and the different Swedish rhythms of life.' What's more, in Sweden Maramotti met the girl who four months ago became the mother of his twin daughters. In one of our email exchanges, he told me that the whole family, dog included, was heading from Sweden to Italy by car. Considering the overall tone of his visual world, it is not difficult to understand why, in a fast-transportation era, he decided on this old-fashioned and slower way of travelling...

— *When did you approach photography for the first time?* My father was a black and white amateur photographer. From him I learnt the basics of photography: apertures, times, focus and so on. When in Paris, I considered being a photographer as an option. I started going to my two favourite photo bookstores almost every day. I decided what I like in photography, and I was trying to understand if photography has rules or specific ways to express itself.

— *Did you have any specific training in photography?* No... And I miss not having an education in a good art school. I would say that to learn how to take a photograph is simple. I think an art school would have given me a better culture in contemporary art and, more than anything, the possibility to confront and share my work, my projects and my ideas with professors and other students.

— *Most of your series are inspired by places like Sweden, Italy and Iceland. Is photography a form of 'geographical' exploration for you?* It is, but everything came almost by itself: I work for an image bank and I am forced to keep the images in a very precise order based on locations. Eventually I liked this way of creating a thread for my photos. A geographical order often transcends the meaning of the single images and helps me to remember, like a visual and very personal journal.

— *There is always a sort of natural atmospheric light in your photographs that makes them look in between ancient and timeless...* I try to escape objective photographs, and I don't like pure reportages. For that, there are photographers better than me. What you see in my images is often what I would have liked to see when I was there. I like to show my impressions and I look for my colours. I often don't like high contrasts, and in postproduction I take away high saturations. If I take a picture of a landscape I avoid lights I don't like, and maybe because of that my images look like you said.

— *Where did you take the photographs for your series Honey and Ochre?* Two years ago I made a summer trip to Iceland. The idea was to fly fish brown trout in streams. I gave up when I saw the extreme nature of the island: no trees, a cold desert, strong and wild waters. I was amazed, so I decided to take images always in overexposure to emphasize the feeling of being on another planet or at the end of the world. Back home, I played more in the postproduction to reach the feeling I'd had there. In *Honey* I wanted to give the impression of Mars like it was pictured in the '50s and '60s. *Ochre* was definitely inspired by the photography of the first part of 2001 A Space Odyssey.

— *I am particularly curious about some of your still lifes... the one with the giraffes and the other with the okapi... what's the story with them?* When I lived in Paris I often went to the two zoos of the city. I always felt sad and impotent watching the sadness and the frustration of the animals captured there but somehow I was also attracted by that old stupid way of keeping the wilderness. The giraffes probably were a couple or siblings or simply friends, separated by that thin wall you see in the pictures. The okapi was alone – forever I supposed. The fake painted trees behind them were there as a decoy to make us think that we were in the jungle and everything was fine for them. I took the picture of this bizarre cruelty.

— *Why are flora and fauna among your favourite subjects?* Trees, animals, flowers and meadows have been there before me and they will be there after my existence. With photography I witness my time with a personal point of view: the colour of a flower, the majesty of trees – that is what I want to preserve. They will never be the same! Did you ever walk in a big forest? Here in Scandinavia I do it often, and every time I feel like all the sounds and all the smells are new: things to discover, animals to spy and places to explore. Maybe it is also a way to recall my childhood, when I was looking for hedgehogs or big insects.

— *What are your future projects?* I will be in Italy for the next three weeks to visit my parents. I want to make a work about them and their decadent house, where I grew up. For me, maybe for them as well, but most importantly, for my kids.

www.ruggeromaramotti.com

Untitled, 2008, film negative

Untitled, 2011, digital

Untitled, 2001, film negative

Untitled, 2009, digital

Untitled, 2009, digital

With photography I witness my time
with a personal point of view: the
colour of a flower, the majesty of trees
– that is what I want to preserve.
They will never be the same! Did you
ever walk in a big forest?

Untitled, 2010, film negative

Hiro Kurata

BATS
&
BRUSHES

By Ana Ibarra

Hiro Kurata grew up in Tokyo and Chicago and the influences of each culture can be recognized in his work. Sumo wrestlers, baseball players and samurai warriors fight in a surreal virtual space of bright pastel colours. Changing the ordinary environment of these characters, Kurata manages to create a different understanding: the baseball player becomes a warrior, the samurai a sportsman, the surreal becomes real.

— *You were born in Japan, but moved back and forth to Chicago when you were little. Have the cultural differences influenced who you are today?* My family moved from Japan to Chicago for few years in 1987. I never noticed how those years of growing up in a foreign culture had affected me until I looked back after a decade or two. The cultural differences between the East and the West of course had the biggest impact. But the nature in the suburbs imprinted itself on me with great nostalgia. Humongous playgrounds and fields, the falling leaves of a big oak tree in autumn, the silence and the whiteout in a snow storm, sunset over the Great Lake. All these memories taught me something very special, universal, which might be hard to explain in words.

— *What are the things that surprised you most when moving?* What I really struggled and had a hard time with was my Tokyo days after those wonderful years in Chicago. Some kids couldn't accept the new kid in town who spoke English and brought peanut butter and jelly sandwiches for lunch. Above all, I couldn't cope with being the 'special one'. In Japan, we have a saying: 'the nail that sticks out gets hammered down', and that was exactly what happened. I did not have enough guts to stand up and be myself. It took me a long time and I made a big effort to adjust to the new environment and the people. As the years went by, I fitted in the crowd. I was playing sports and Nintendo games, just like any of the other kids on the block. But, I guess, I knew that I was leaving something important behind, and come to think about it, this abasement experience may have been my motivation towards a creative career.

— *Did you study painting?* After spending some harsh years in Tokyo, I was able to come back to an American high school. I was always interested in making things, challenging myself in the creative world, and I ended up in New York. It was 1999 when I entered the Parsons School of Design to earn my bachelor degree in illustration. Thinking back, I do regret not having studied fine arts painting, but then I wasn't sure of what I wanted to do, or where I wanted to go. We did have some painting classes in my course, but it was more narrative and editorial illustration painting, which I wasn't really into. I was more interested in counter culture – art that would relate to the youth culture of skating and punk rock. One of the best things was to be in Jordin Isip's class. I was not the kind of guy who would talk a lot in the class, meaning that I didn't really speak with him directly, but I learned a lot from his attitude towards creation, which felt serious and honest. That was the time when I started to be more passionate about making art.

— *Where do the surreal elements in your work come from?* The world is filled with recognizable icons. We scan things in and categorize them to know what they are, and I often underestimate the hidden beauty behind them. By editing and replacing a recognizable icon into a different context, our mind can rediscover them and create new ideas. I have been obsessed with painting striped uniformed baseball players for nearly ten years. It started out quite unconsciously. I guess I needed some hero to show up over and over again, so my paintings would someday form a sequential story.

— *Why do you often represent violence?* It is out of a fearful curiosity. I hate violence, but at the same time I am very interested in it. Human history has always dealt with violence and sorrow. It is so raw and real I am scared of it. That's why I represent it; to show my perspective of it, and here comes the baseball slugger... The slugger I paint often represents a strong fearless figure, physically and mentally. He is trained and built for slamming the ball, but in time of need he also has the ability to fight against someone or something. Can aggression and calmness coexist? I think so. The key is not to just sit around and sing a happy song ignoring the world around you, but to have the option of fighting back against something that messes with your peace.

— *What have been your main influences?* It's hard to keep track, but definitely my childhood experiences, nature, comic books and music. As a member of the Japanese manga generation now grown up, I would like to introduce one of my favourite manga titles: *Phoenix* by Osamu Tezuka. It is a series of twelve books written between 1967 and 1988. Tezuka has written over seven hundred manga books, and what he considered as his life's work was this spectacular series about time, life and death.

— *Do you have a regular routine?* I am a semi full-time artist, meaning I sometimes work for someone else. I work as an assistant for a NY based sculptor named Forrest Myers. He is a sophisticated and well-established artist and I get inspired just being with him. So for me it is more than just a job. I learn a lot from him, how an artist's life is lead, or should be lead. The other days, I do my own work.

www.shiloku.com

When mother was young, 2011 Acrylic on wood panel, 76 x 61 cm,

Greek Myth 09, 2009, acrylic on wood panel, 128 x128 cm

Can aggression
and calmness coexist?
I think so

III

ART & CRAFT:
AN EMBROIDERED
WEB

Margherita Dessanay
discusses the use of embroidery
in contemporary art

FOLLOWING THE THREAD

Maurizio Anzeri, *Round Midnight*, 2009, Embroidery on Print, 62 x 45 cm, Courtesy the artist, Saatchi Gallery

Traditionally categorized as 'decorative art', or labelled 'arts and crafts', embroidery offers artists unexpected and varied possibilities: while stimulating their creative process, it can produce distinctive results. More and more artists work with this technique. 'I think there is a really wonderful community of people right now using textiles and sewing in very interesting ways, though thematically there is a huge range of work. I feel part of this community because of my medium,' says American artist Lauren DiCioccio.

Wikipedia defines embroidery as 'the art or handicraft of decorating fabric or other materials with needle and thread or yarn', touching upon the dichotomy between the purely technical aspects of it (the craft) and the aesthetic potentialities that it can open up (the art).

This separation is widely accepted when discussing art or craft. Both are perceived as different and mutually exclusive universes; art belonging to the high domain of culture, and craft left at the 'lower' level, a utilitarian and decorative activity.

'Art is held in much higher regard than craft,' embroidery artist Inge Jacobsen confesses. 'I have been told that my work has too much of a "craft aspect" about it, as a bad thing. Perhaps it is because craft is largely viewed as something you do for a hobby. It can be frustrating when craft magazines ask me for a "how-to" guide so that their readers can spruce up their holiday photos. I'm not doing this for the sake of doing it – I have my reasons.'

What are these reasons? How do the threads of craft and art weave themselves together in the practices of a noticeable number of contemporary artists, with surprisingly fresh and original visual results?

PATIENTLY SETTING
THE TAMBOUR

In practical terms, embroidery consists of decorating a piece of fabric, or another support, by sewing upon it after it has been placed around the tambour [the circular frame that holds the fabric]. It is a skill that needs practice and manual mastery. There was a time when it was a compulsory subject for girls at school – as it still was, for example, for half-Danish, half-Irish Inge Jacobsen. Hinke Schreuders can trace back her first memory of embroidery to her primary school in The Netherlands. Later, she improved her practice by making clothes for herself and her sister. Maria Ikonomopoulou remembers how her personal background in Greece was full of embroidery and other kinds of textile works: 'I've always been surrounded by women like my grandmothers, mother and my older sister who could make miracles with thread and textile. In my neighbourhood women were often sitting together in the afternoon hours.' Embroidery is traditionally a feminine craft, even if it is now often adopted by men. For many of the artists who now use embroidery in their works, it evokes domestic memories, with mothers and grandmothers intent in the making. The conscious choice of using it with an artistic purpose often derives from the homely environment, and is rarely part of any institutional art training.

For the London-based Italian artist Maurizio Anzeri, who has been influenced by (and has collaborated with) the fashion world, using threads and hand-stitching was always part of his practice. But it wasn't until he fused it with his passion for old photographs that embroidery became a deliberate expressive tool. One day, while working on a series of black ink drawings with fine Japanese shapes reminiscent of embroidery, Anzeri, out of boredom, started working with a thread on the photographs.

Maurizio Anzeri, *Lacrimosa*, 2009, Embroidery on Print, 62 x 45 cm, Courtesy the artist, Private Collection

Maurizio Anzeri, *Marcel*, 2011, Embroidery on Photo, 23 x 17,8 cm, Courtesy the artist, Saatchi Collection

'When I went to the studio the day after, something clicked,' he told the online magazine *Don't Panic*.

Ehren Elizabeth Reed had to face her own internalized prejudice about art being of a higher order of magnitude than craft: 'While at art school studying painting, I maintained a somewhat latent desire to incorporate sewing and embroidery into my work. I had a natural affinity for these materials and wanted to bring them into my painting practice, yet I had a difficult time integrating these two media. I believe I was still under the misapprehension that painting was the highest form of fine art, and that the materials I wanted to use were still confined to the world of "craft". When, in the last year of my course of study, I began using found imagery, maps and books in my work, all of them seemed particularly well-suited to sewing and embroidery. At that point, I essentially abandoned painting as my medium in favour of something that was a more natural mode of expression for me – my true and intuitive voice.'

Ehren Elizabeth Reed, *Consolidation 3*, 2010, mixed media, 10,2 × 45,7 cm

Embroidery has drifted into the practice of many artists almost by chance, as a resource you never purposefully cultivate and almost forget that you have. For instance, Jacobsen was studying fine art in a very open course and she wanted to work with images collected from magazines such as *Vogue*, *i-D* and *Dazed & Confused*. Still uncertain about what to do with them, she was trawling through a pound shop when she 'found a pack of twenty different coloured threads, so I thought about using them instead of ink and paint.'

There wasn't any deliberate, conscious intention when Shaun Kardinal started using needle and thread. 'I started sewing up images a few years ago, after receiving a piece in the mail from a friend. I had been trading small works via mail, experimenting with collage and printmaking. In response to her embroidered collage, I cut up a few old postcards I'd recently purchased, and set about reassembling them with some thread I had. Enjoying the process, I made a few more to send to other friends. Soon, I was making them for no one, just enjoying the craft of it.'

The slow nature of the act of embroidery – the making of – is generally perceived as a private pleasure. 'Before attempting them, I would never have guessed that I would find so much pleasure in these embroidered works,' Kardinal confides. New York-based artist Melissa Zexter defines embroidery as a respite from the chaos of living in a big city. It first happened 'by accident'. The artist had already worked for ten years with mixed media and photography when, in 1999 – while working on disassembling photographs before re-

With embroidery, I have to contemplate most decisions before actually trying them because of the simple fact that it just takes a long time

Hinke Schreuders

assembling them in a sort of mosaic – she ran out of photographs. Necessity is the mother of invention, and Melissa decided to make her own handmade paper and sew simple images on it. 'I liked the sewn "drawings" on paper. The way I sew is similar to the way I draw, with a lot of attention to details, and in small sections.' For Stacey Page, the act of embroidering resembles that of drawing: it is a slow process through which an image is created. 'It is paying attention to points and straight lines that allows for the basic structure of an embroidered image as well as for details such as forging a curve,' she says. 'The process is very similar to a slow drawing; connecting the spaces between two points.'

Slowness is also what makes the difference, and drives Hinke Schreuders to use embroidery as a better means of expression than, say, painting or drawing: 'I found that when drawing or painting, it was too easy to go past the point where a work or image is just right. With embroidery, I have to contemplate most decisions before actu-

Inge Jacobsen, *Partly stitched Chanel Advert*, 2010, 20.5cm x 28.5cm

www.chanel.com

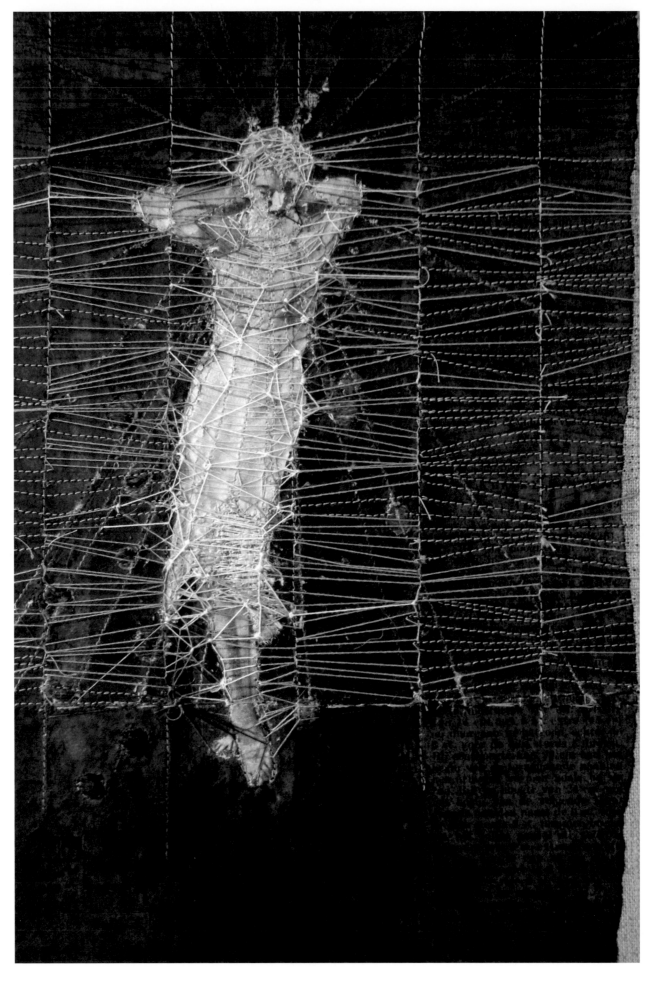

Hinke Schreuders, works on paper #19, 2010, yarn and ink on paper on canvas, 25 x 15 x 5,5 cm

ally trying them because of the simple fact that it just takes a long time'. Maurizio An-zeri agrees: 'When I begin the stitching, something else happens; drawing will never do what thread will – the light changes, and at some points you can lose the face [the artist uses photographic portraits as subjects in his work], and at other moments you can still see under it.'

Time, concentration and solitude are key factors in releasing the creative potential of embroidery. Maria Ikonomopoulou admits that the time required for making an embroidered piece always makes her nervous. 'But I like it. I can think very well during the embroidery process. I do have a plan before starting, but the embroidery itself always pushes me in new directions.'

This reminds me of an anecdote I associate with the work *The Great English Letter Writers* by Lauren DiCioccio. Jane Austen and the Bronte Sisters would hide their writing under their needle-work and that the monotonous and repetitive act of sewing encouraged the free flights of their imagination. DiCioccio agrees with this, 'I definitely find handiwork to be meditative and soothing. I think of a lot of my ideas for new projects during the creation process – the tedious monotony of the sewing allows me to be just distracted enough for my mind to wander in creative ways.'

I remember my discomfort with the answer an artist once gave me. Asked about the material skills required for realizing a quilt he created, he replied to me that, *of course*, he *hadn't* materially realized the work. He made the design for the quilt and then gave it to be executed by some 'needle-professionals'. This memory, and my feeling of unresolved disappointment with the answer, comes now as a telling example of the attitude of a certain part of the art-world. According to this faction, art and creativity reside, and express themselves fully, only in the mind as an idea. The skill and the craft for materially realizing it are a secondary moment – something better left to the hand of some 'skilled professionals'. This is a path that was opened to artists from 'Duchampian' times, and I wouldn't have a problem with it were it not for the fact that there seems to be an established scale of value attached to it: the mind comes first, and drives the body. It would not make any difference if the body in question were that of the artist. Mind and body seem to be commonly understood as separate 'agents' in creative terms, with an implied supremacy of the first over the second. But such stark categorization risks overshadowing the importance of that constant creative flow between the mind and the body, which is not a one-way street.

Although Stacey Page works with a machine, she thinks it is important to create a relationship with that machine. 'It allows for an intimate relationship with the work. With such a short needle, the skill is then close to the body and mind or idea.' The experience and words of the artists involved with thread and needle shed a new light upon the importance of connecting mind and body in an almost 'holistic' physical relation. The craft involved in this relationship is not just a 'hobby' type skill, but a vital, active clog in the mechanics of artistic creation.

'Doing everything by hand is both my favourite and least favourite part of embroidery,' says Inge Jacobsen. 'It can be very frustrating because it takes so long to stitch a whole page. I am always thinking of other pieces I would like to make, but I always feel guilty about leaving one piece to start another...' Yet, it is this apparent paradox in the practice that feeds and drives her creativity: 'It's difficult not being able to make them faster and moving on to something new, but it does help me stay focused and weed out the good ideas from the bad. I will remember the good ideas, but the bad ones are, hopefully, forgotten.'

INTERWEAVING MIND
AND BODY

Another creative trigger, in artistic terms, is the symbolic value that the thread and the act of embroidering conjure. The gesture and tools naturally drive visual themes and concepts in open and unexpected ways. A thread is essentially a tool of connection, allowing imaginative associations to become visual evidence. In the work of Dutch artist Berend Strik, inanimate landscapes are colourfully animated. As a result of the embroidered intervention, the inorganic world of architectures harmoniously merges with nature. Objects appear alive and active just like human beings by means of the physical and metaphorical interconnections it establishes. Maria Ikonomopoulou says that when discovering the soft three-dimensionality of the embroidery relief, she realized the conceptual meaning of using a thread as a physical and metaphorical sign. 'The question that connects all my works as "a red thread" is if it is possible to combine collectivity and individualism in our time and how.' For her series *Spaces Between Us*,

Hinke Schreuders, works on paper #16, 2010, yarn and ink on paper on canvas, 25 x 17 x 5,5 cm

Berend Strik, *Natural Order, Architecture*, 2005, embroidered picture, 30,5 x30,5 cm

Shaun Kardinal, *Strings over Strasbourg*, 2011, hand-embroidered postcard, 10,2 x 15,2 cm

Melissa Zexter, *Girl On Rock*, 2011, gelatin silver print, thread, 50.8 x 60.96 cm

Ikonomopoulou selects images featuring mostly two people, taken from the daily press. Questioning the essence of the space that separates these two people, she fills it with red embroidery, thus making it an active agent in the relationship.

Images from the daily press have also inspired Lauren DiCioccio for her series *Sewnnews*. When she started using embroidery in 2005, she was working around the theme of 'the newspaper', attempting to figure out what she wanted to capture about it. 'One day, I decided to sew an edition of the newspaper into a quilt. I felt that the piece was very successful and I decided that using a technique rooted in craft was the most appropriate way to talk about the medium of the daily newspaper and its potential obsolescence. I'm using a technique that is associated with the past while making works about media objects that soon will become old-fashioned. I'm interested in using the tactility of cloth and the poignancy of labour-intensive handiwork to spark a human connection to the viewers of my work. I think recreating these images in the medium of embroidery allows the viewers to reconsider an image that they might otherwise overlook. Seeing these objects and images recreated with time and care and attention begs a viewer to ask why so much time is being applied to these images and then to rethink the materials and his or her relation to them.' Similarly, Ehren Elizabeth Reed considers the handcrafting aspect of the process as incredibly important, not just in formal but also conceptual terms: 'Much of the source imagery in my work is developed digitally and the hand-hewn physicality of the stitching serves as an important conceptual counterpoint to the digital imagery. In my early embroidered works, I began to develop a visual language that was essentially the reinterpretation of pixels using thread. This language, in a more refined form, has become a consis-

Hand sewing alters time. It allows me to react to a moment – the photograph and alter and adjust the memory

Melissa Zexter

tent theme throughout my work.' Nowadays, the source material for her work are images that Reed selects from found photographs and old school yearbooks. Once the image is selected, modified and transferred onto new surfaces, she embroiders on it. 'I find that embroidering upon existing images creates a dialogue between the two, introducing a three-dimensional, tactile and distinctly physical element to imagery that can feel flat, distant or remote. The images I use recall the past and refer to people or histories that are but memories for which no physical markers remain. The stitching upon these images serves to highlight this disjuncture, yet also to bring these narratives closer to the viewer by showcasing the implicit touch of the human hand.'

For many of the artists interviewed, photography works as the tambour for their needlework. They do not simply decorate or cover the image. Melissa Zexter explains, 'I start with a recognizable image and then superimpose sewing over it. Embroidery is a reaction to the photographs and is a process that aids the transformation and transcendence of identity of the person or place being photographed.' Working on her own photographic shoots, she feels that photographs have the power to stop time and become a document of the past. 'Hand sewing alters time. It allows me to react to a moment – the photograph – and alter and adjust the memory'. It is a re-activation of the subject in new terms, and leading to a new experience of it. There is no better word for it than the one used by Stacey Page: resurrection; in new terms and with a different meaning.

Inge Jacobsen, *Partly Sewn Image of Lily Donaldson from British Vogue Magazine – 2009*, 2010, 22cm x 28.5cm

PARIS

Lily Donaldson models a little
black dress by Jean Paul
Gaultier, photographed by
Patrick Demarchelier, 2009

Shaun Kardinal, *Alteration n. 28*, 2011, hand-embroidered postcard, 14 x 8.9 cm

Shaun Kardinal, *Alteration n. 12*, 2011, hand-embroidered postcard, 14 x 8.9 cm

Shaun Kardinal, *Alteration n. 32*, 2011, hand-embroidered postcard, 14 x 11,4 cm

Shaun Kardinal, *Alteration n. 1*, 2011, hand-embroidered postcard, 24,1 x 11,4 cm

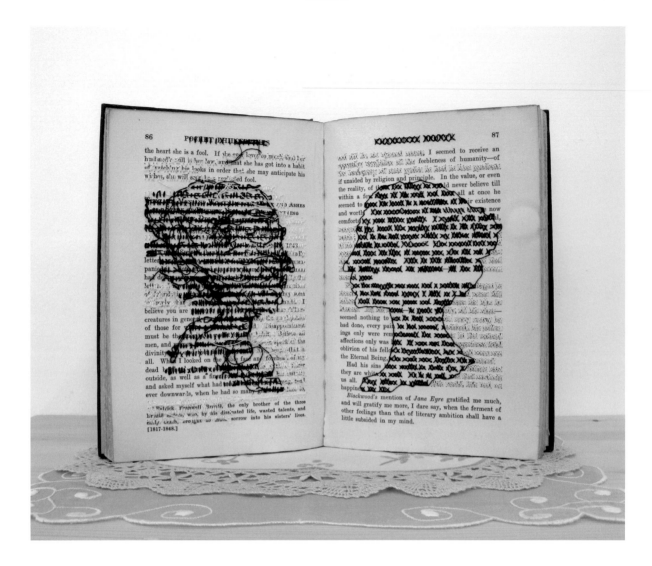

Lauren DiCioccio, *The Great English Letter Writers*, 2009,
Cross-stitch into found book, 30.48 x 17.78 cm

Lauren DiCioccio, *19 MAR 10 (Barack Obama and Hilary Clinton)*,
2010, hand-embroidery on cotton muslin over the March 19,
2010 issue of the New York Times, 29.8 x 29.2 cm

The poetics of Maurizio Anzeri's photo-sculptures (as he likes to call them) reside in the very act of inserting a needle into a pre-existing image. For him, it is a proper act of penetration through which embroidery 'feeds' the image. 'I try to never completely cover a face, you can always still see the face underneath. There are no rules other than I always leave one or both eyes open. It's like a mask – not a mask you put on, but something that grows out of you.' Like Maurizio Anzeri, Stacey Page works on anonymous old photographic portraits that raise questions of 'status, avatar, identity, fashion, evolution'. Adding thread to them is the specific response that she feels the original photograph desires. 'There are recurring hints of crowns, masks, mutations or developments,' she explains.

Inge Jacobsen starts with images from high-end fashion magazines as well as pornographic images: 'I tried to think of ways to experiencing the magazine other than just reading it, or looking at it. I wanted to get under its skin. The stitching has allowed me to do that. It's been my way of intervening in the exclusive world of high fashion magazines, partly by giving it a very touchable surface. More importantly, by removing the glossy surface and replacing it with a cloth surface, I give the image a homely and less glamorous aspect. The cross stitching has allowed me to make mass produced magazines unique.'

For Hinke Schreuders, embroidery has historically implied something about the social condition of women; their relegation to the domestic sphere and in a 'decorative', secondary role. 'I want to explore if and how those implications still work through in my generation. I try to understand how I differ from, for example, my mother, who was a young woman in the 1950s. In concrete terms, this means that I'm getting my inspiration from 1950s magazines, from old embroidery patterns, as well as from porn and modern female culture. I try to alter the image with my interventions, to distill a different meaning or atmosphere from it. With my additions, I try to show hidden layers that may be in the picture. The mostly one-dimensional pictures of fashion models are made ambivalent by my interventions.'

UNRAVELING THE PREJUDICE

Hinke Schreuders finds that, 'embroidery is the perfect mix between 2D and 3D work, in the sense of dealing with composition: the image – and material: the needle and thread.' She also admits that she was embarrassed about telling people that she made art with embroidery, 'expecting them to think that it was dull.' This feeling is at the core of her expressive and thematic choices. 'I used to add that I don't do it in a traditional way, that is to say, neatly, and that it depicts erotic images – as a counterweight.'

If the artist still feels the need to justify her work, I wonder how strong the prejudice against craft and skill as legitimate co-leading actors in the act of artistic production is. Last year I attended an exhibition of the textile works of Louise Bourgeois. I went there with a friend who is passionate about and professionally involved in the art world. The delicate and intimate tone of the pieces brought to my mind the image of old Louise Bourgeois, sitting in a chair, fingers constantly in motion, poetically immersed in the making of them. It was such a fresh and humanly 'normal' image, put against the social hustle and bustle surrounding the figure of the contemporary artist and the art world in general. When I shared this feeling with my friend, she replied, as if stating the obvious: 'But *of course* Louise Bourgeois didn't make them. She created the design for it!'

Again, that 'of course'… That old and unsolved '*of course*' resonates now as the tangled knot, the crux, of my discomfort. Do we take for granted now, as fact, that creativity is only a pure act of the mind, so much so that the image of a great artist intent in a craft sounds naïve and unlikely?

Defining art is a complicated business, a richly nuanced Penelope's web made of many interweaving threads. One of them is the idea that it develops in the mind of the artist. But there are other important nuances contributing to the incessant power of art to originally renew itself and the world around it.

'A traditional difference between art and craft could be that the art making process follows the idea of the artist while craft making processes follow the sensibility of the craftsman for his material' Maria Ikonomopoulou says. The word 'handicraft' alternatively used for defining embroidery is a compound of craft and hand. Scientific studies remind us of the paramount role of the hand in the physical, cultural and social evolution of humankind from primates. According to them, the evolution of the

Maria Ikonomopoulou, *Intimacy*, 2007, print, embroidery on canvas, 100 x 80 cm

Stacey Page, Nicole, 2011, thread on found photograph, 12.7 x 17.8 cm

brain has run parallel (and has depended upon) the physical evolution of the articulations of the hand and the new activities it made possible. Similarly, let's consider all the creative potentialities and artistic drifts explored and developed by these artists through the 'simple' act of stitching with a thread. I believe it is worth reconsidering, in less obvious terms, the parallel dialectics of creativity involving ideas and manual skills. Shaun Kardinal sums it up as: 'Art is an implemented abstract, while craft is a practice. Great artists employ an exceeding amount of both.'

Against that still unconvincing 'of course', it is refreshing to hear Kardinal say: 'For years, I wanted to be Seattle's Art Don – always connecting and being connected. In my time here, I have been involved in nearly every element of the community. I've delved deeply into the art world and would not be who I am today without it. I am thankful for the experiences and opportunities it has provided, not to mention fortunate to have met so many amazing people within it. These days, however, I am more often content to enjoy a night in, sewing alongside my girl, avoiding the myriad trappings of the art world, and simply honing a craft...' At least it makes everything less obvious. And for the sake of accuracy, I'd like to point out that Louise Bourgeoise did, as I later found out, *of course* make her own embroidered pieces with her own knobby old hands.

Ehren Elizabeth Reed, Consolidation 2, 2010, mixed media 55.9 x 55.9 cm

Melissa Zexter, Nurse, 2010, gelatin silver print, thread, oil, 50.8 x 60.96 cm

Maria Ikonomopoulou, *Bo(o)men*, 2007, embroidery, print on canvas, 20 x 15 cm

ON THE CUTTING EDGE BETWEEN
DESIGN, CRAFTS, FASHION,
ART AND ARCHITECTURE

OBJECT
ROTTERDAM

LAS PALMAS, LP 11   WILHELMINAKADE 326   3072 AP ROTTERDAM

9–12 FEBRUARY

NEW PARTICIPANTS, NEW PARTNERS, NEW PROGRAM

WWW.OBJECTROTTERDAM.COM

IV

Contact, 2011, oil on canvas, 65 cm x 58 cm

Benjamin Rubloff

Text by Katya Tylevich
Photography by Claudio Campo-Garcia

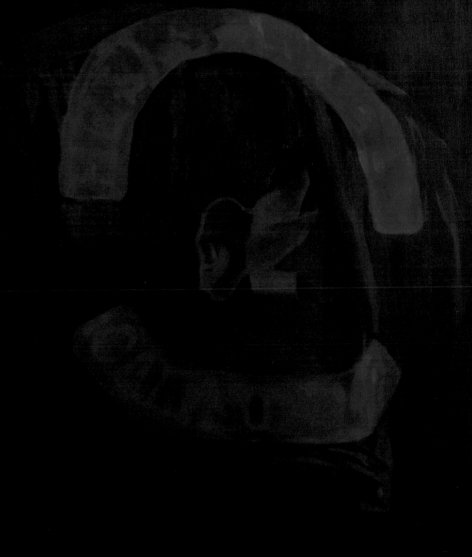

Altamont, 2010 oil on paper, wood, reflective glass, 137cm x 109cm

SPACE OF ENGAGEMENT

More than a year ago, I met Benjamin Rubloff by chance at an art exhibit at the Contemporary Fine Arts in Berlin. We talked on the terrace overlooking Museum Island until the place emptied and we were asked to leave. At the time, I was doing a series of interviews with Berlin artists and designers, and Rubloff played into my paranoid delusion that everybody in Berlin is an artist. Rubloff was then finishing up an MFA at Cornell University in Ithaca, NY. He could no longer say he was 'in Berlin' with perfect accuracy, though he'd lived there for several years prior, and was looking forward to moving back.

We didn't exchange cards, numbers, or even Facebook invites. But there are other ways to stalk an artist online, you know. I followed Rubloff's drawings and paintings as they mushroomed on his website, and I read into the lonely spaces of his works — sometimes incorrectly (well, 'incorrectly' in quotation marks) it turns out; something I discovered when I finally caught up with Rubloff again, as he was driving from Ithaca to Boston, in the process of relocating back to Berlin. Since we'd last met, Rubloff had finished his MFA, and was now in the middle of packing boxes, and packing more boxes. Very good. There's no more exciting time to talk to a person than when he has no time to talk. Rubloff and I picked up from where we'd left off.

— *How did you end up in Berlin, in the first place?*
Back in 1998, I was living in San Francisco and had saved up money to escape the States and travel to Eastern Europe. I was vaguely planning to live out there for a while. I planned to hitchhike from Amsterdam to Poland, but a couple from Berlin gave me a ride and insisted that I come see their city. It was one of those transformative travel experiences. I managed to find a friend I'd made in Seattle years before who was from East Berlin, and for a few days she drove me all over the city on a motorcycle. I saw Potsdamer Platz, which was then this enormous, theatrical construction site. And there were all these amazing informal kinds of places that had begun popping up around the city, which were really like nothing I had ever seen before. I thought about staying and was even offered a job playing music there, but I left because I was just beginning this trip I had been planning for so long, and I was really hungry to see more. I ended up settling in Granada, Spain that year, but when I returned to the States, I started thinking about moving to Berlin. It took five years, but I did finally move there in 2004. Then, after five years in Berlin, I felt a need to get out and get some fresh perspective on things, so I went back to the States to do an MFA. Now I'm returning to Berlin for what I imagine will be another significant stretch.

— *What's driving you back?*
I am productive there in a way that stems from some degree of isolation: it's a city where I can still be a complete stranger and go for long stretches of uninterrupted work. But when I want to go out, there is always something interesting to see and a contagious energy that accompanies things. I have a great community of artists there, as well. The people I know there are really engaged in their work and I get a lot from just talking with them — a lot of them aren't even visual artists.

— *What's your abridged autobiography, outside of Berlin?*
I grew up in the suburbs of New York City. In college, I floated around a lot, until I finished with a degree in American Studies from Wesleyan University. During college, I focused my energy on writing — I really wanted to be a fiction writer, but I struggled with sitting still at the computer every morning. Immediately after college I was working as a cook and playing jazz in bars. I guess it's pretty clear that there was a lot of floating around back then. Later, I became a public school teacher in Boston, where I worked on a number of documentary projects with teenagers. I didn't really start painting seriously until I was in my late twenties.

— *Was that a romantic moment in your life: you finally knew you were going to be an artist?*
It was never a romantic thing, really. It actually took me a long time to call myself an artist — largely *because* of those romantic associations. It evolved pretty organically, though: everything I had done before I began painting worked its way into how I approach my work. It's informed not only the references, but also what I want from a painting and how I expect it to function.

— *What was your idea of an artist before you actually called yourself one?*
I was incredibly lucky to have a great art teacher in high school who communicated to all of her students that art was a radically open way of engaging with the world. I think it took me a long time to be able understand it that way, but I think that idea was always there. Making things and responding to things was always an important part of my engagement with the world. Even as a kid, I remember being really caught up with my experience of things. I suppose I always knew I would be making something.

— *Do you consider yourself an 'American' artist? It's an adjective that comes up in what's written about you. Also, many of your subjects are geographically American, and series like* Ecologies *or* This is a Wilderness *seem to bottle an atmosphere and stillness specific to the lonely stretches of America.*
What's funny is that work was often seen as American in Berlin, but when I went to the U.S. for graduate school it was seen as European. Still, I see my work as American insofar as I have been preoccupied with ideas about American mythologies for a long time. So there is certainly a good deal of cultural specificity in the set of references that I respond to, but I also feel that those references have expanded, as American culture has been so widely disseminated, especially

in the post 9/11 era when its anxieties have become infectious. In that way, I think that talking about art as American, German, or whatever has really begun to loose traction.

It's interesting you mention *Ecologies*, though, because that's a series of paintings based on German allotment gardens. But you see it as having a specifically American quality. Maybe there is something about the way I process subjects that is informed by an American idea of space, that is still and contemplative, and that also lends itself to the kind of economy that you get in the writing of Raymond Carver, or Stephen Shore's work in *American Surfaces*. Their works have been really important for me. I think I respond specifically to the idea of an expansive space that also has the potential to collapse or refuse access. It's an interesting contradiction about space in the American imagination. I've increasingly come to think about American conceptions of space in terms of territories that are invested with notions of secrecy and privacy. In the last year and a half, my work has moved away from landscape, but these issues of space are still there. In a way, the move away from a more explicit topographical kind of space has opened up possibilities to think about space more conceptually. It's pushed me to think more about the space of engagement, about the viewer's experience of that space.

— *Did you consciously move away from landscapes?*
It was surprising. I just couldn't really get behind the work anymore; it felt too illustrative somehow, which seems to always be a struggle in painting. In retrospect, I think I was able to do a lot of that landscape work in Berlin, because the references were more distant.

Once I moved to upstate New York, I was immersed in a place where there is a very different relationship to the landscape than the one I had growing up in suburbs of the city. In the suburbs, nature was a kind of periphery; it was a space apart where a lot of transgressive kinds of things happened. But upstate, it was a different reality — the specificity of it made it harder to work with. The psychological and mythological dimensions that interested me seemed less accessible. So I guess I had to move on to other subject matter to get at the things that had interested me in the landscape work.

— *Are the settings in your paintings 'real' places — have you been to them?*
Very few works are based on firsthand experience. I work from images. I search through archives to see what resonates. I'm especially interested in how that resonance occurs when the images are removed from their original context. I have boxes and boxes of images, and have spent more

Zone, 2009, oil on canvas, 80 x 100 cm

and more time collecting images online in the last several years. I find it incredible that out of this increasingly fast stream of images, some still rise up and resonate in unsuspecting ways. Once I locate an image, I can become quite obsessive about it. I work slowly, often painting it over and over again, trying out different approaches until it takes on a form that has a particular effect that brought me to the image in the first place.

Of course, nothing ever goes where I expect it will. I try to plan my work — I do a lot of looking around until a series comes into a kind of partial view. But so much happens in the studio. I back myself into a corner, get frustrated, or fail miserably at an intention and then something emerges from that. It's maybe a brutal way of working, or at the least, a punishing way, but it's almost always the outliers and impulsive works that become the most significant for me.

— *Do you ever think of your works in terms of narrative, of fiction and nonfiction?*

I am actually really interested in ideas about narration. My work certainly engages with the expectation of narrative, though I've sought to undermine that a bit. Narrative is interesting for me when it challenges viewers to become aware of their desire for narrative, for coherence and meaning.

In my most recent works, I'm thinking about how constellations of paintings can provide a kind of loose scaffolding for entering the work, though I think about it less in terms of narrative these days and more in terms of correspondences, or image relations. As for fiction or nonfiction? I guess painting is always a kind of fiction. But when it's really working, I think it functions more like poetry, in that it can point in so many directions at the same time.

My work has moved away from landscape, but these issues of space are still there

— In 2009, you co-founded an artist collective called La Chose. What is it, exactly?
The idea started from sharing a studio with two Berlin artists: Julien Rouvroy and Betti Scholz. After days in the studio, we would often go to exhibitions together and spend a lot of time talking about the problems of exhibition, and im-agining the kinds of exhibitions that we would find more interesting. After a lot of long nights like this, we simply got tired of talking about it and started putting the thing into action. I think it would have become insufferable otherwise. Suddenly, it wasn't an abstraction, but a kind of imperative.

We were interested in collaborating on large group exhibitions that would directly engage with the sites where they occur. That's a great thing about working in Berlin: there are all these incredible spaces with different histories that pose really interesting challenges for exhibition. In the process of putting on our first large exhibition at an abandoned bathhouse in 2009, we met a lot of artists who shared similar interests. I am really excited about the work we do together. It takes on such a different kind of energy than the solitude of a studio practice, and you get a lot of unexpected ideas through the exchange. We meet and work with new artists in each exhibition, and the shift in venues keeps things from getting tired. We are in the process of planning to establish a more permanent home for the collective, where we could also host a residency for international artists who want to come and work in Berlin.

www.lachoseprojects.com
www.benjaminrubloff.com

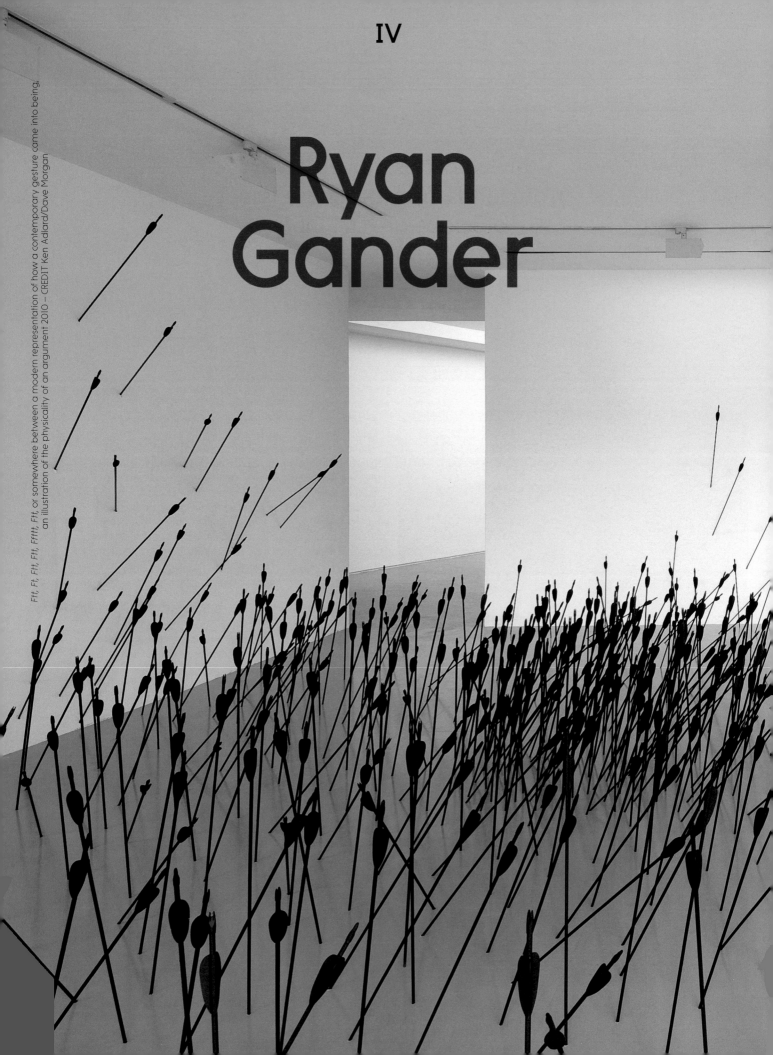

Ryan
Gander

Ftt, Ft, Ftt, Ft, Ftttt, Ft, or somewhere between a modern representation of how a contemporary gesture came into being, an illustration of the physicality of an argument 2010 – CREDIT Ken Adlard/Dave Morgan

A WICKED GAME OF CARDS

Text by Richard Kendrick
Photography by Robin Friend

I am not entirely sure where I am going. I enter the post-code in my mobile phone, and the blue pulsating dot navigates me to my destination. Through huge iron gates, I wander down the East London mews and find the artist in his studio. This is not the first time we have met – that was around seven years ago in the odd surroundings of Manchester Tennis & Racquet Club; a little known private members club, home to one of the few organisations in the country that provide facilities for 'Real Tennis' [the original indoors version of the sport]. I was attending an organised social event in the form of a lecture to slides and sounds.

Ryan Gander was performing the interactive talk titled 'Loose Associations (version 2.1)', dotting between fact and fiction, knocking us (the curious audience) back and forth around a seemingly unrelated court of historical and cultural references and topics such as accents and dialect, J.R.R. Tolkien, London's Barbican Centre and the artist's own grandfather. Now among the UK's foremost young(ish) artists, Gander is still playfully deconstructing and remoulding all aspects of the world as he perceives it, through his diverse way of working. Ryan Gander's ever expanding career combines elements of installation, sculpture, architecture, game play, typography, film, urban planning and design, and he also constructs fine examples of conceptual art using his heightened awareness of experience and the position of objects in his environment.

Gander is an appealing character. His conversation is characterized by a deft and relaxed sense of humour. His meeting table has a pile of cooking books at its centre, and I will later leave with some of his home-grown tomatoes, which have come all the way from Suffolk. After a discussion on the subject of pies, I ask him about his studio and working environment. 'We have been here around a year and a half now, we moved from just over the road. When I say we, I mean the core team. We can do a lot of everything here – everyone has diverse and specialist skills, but we're basically Jacks-of-all-trades. I'll write the content and scripts, and make the decisions throughout the process of creation, and the rest is usually done in-house. We are quite adaptable in terms of what we can do. I work with specialist craftsmen as-and-when needed on certain projects – if we need a professional glass technician or a graphic designer, say.

'The workload isn't really a problem; it is more the decision of what shows to do. If you have spent a lot of time wanting to do shows and exhibitions, then it's hard to say no. Life has been very fast-paced since those days. We are constantly busy now. There are things I can't do, because it is physically impossible to be in two places at once. My colleagues sometimes say I should say no more, as there is the danger of taking on too much and losing focus – and our marbles. It is definitely better to do one good show, rather than three shows that are only half finished.'

The large open space, a converted railway arch, is very ordered. I notice the lack of artwork on show. Gander is quick to pick up on this: 'It's covered up, or stored. I find having art out in the studio a distraction. It's also where the events happen.' The studio space is used for his 'Night School' programme – a monthly informal gathering of salon-style presentation from a host of invited participants. He tells me that 'any idea goes. It's about sharing ideas, being creative. It all feeds off each other. It's similar to a reading week. I enjoy doing them, as they give you a chance to recharge your brain with new information. Listening to other artists, it sets you off on different tangents. You get caught up actually producing things all the time; you don't get a moment to research.'

— Is this why you navigated to London?
No, I ended up here by mistake – because of a girl – not because of art. I wouldn't have come here, I don't think. I had only visited London a handful of times before I eventually moved here, and I was terribly bitter – when I was in Manchester as a student – that I didn't get into BAs and MAs in London.

I always knew I wanted to do something... a job that would be different every day. I definitely wanted to be self-employed, but I didn't really know the possibilities of what art was when I was younger. I was doing art at school like everyone does, but there were people who were better at drawing than me, so I didn't think I would actually work as an artist at that point. Photography came first, and I did art at the same time. I'm not from a family that has anything to do with art. I was never taken to a museum or anything as a kid. Even my parents' friends didn't go to museums – total aspiring-middle-class, red-row-housing-estate-background who were all clones of each other. I had this friend called Max at school who's mum was really arty. I do remember going round there. She was a real artist who made these little paintings. I thought, 'this is good I'd like to do that', but didn't think it would lead down this path.

Another friend – this time whilst I was just completing my BA (for Interactive Arts) in Manchester – said he would

N.. n... n.. nostaggia - (Alchemy Box no 29), 2011 – CREDIT GB Agency

travel round Belgium, Netherlands and Luxemburg looking at post-grad courses. He came back describing them all after doing all the research. So I thought, I better do my MA, or I would to be stuck working in a rubbish job in a freezing warehouse, sewing patches behind holes in jeans so they could be sold on as vintage. Luckily, I got accepted to the Jan van Eyck Akademie in Maastricht, before completing my post-graduate at the Rijksakademie in Amsterdam. It was valuable time. I did consider colleges in London but they would not accept me. I applied to them all, but none would give me an interview.

— Does that make you concerned about the state of art education in our country?
Yes, I guess so, but it's just one of those things. Being centred in the provinces you spend all your time looking at art in magazines and books and not really seeing shows. Back then we – me and friends – would always get hold of the New Contemporary catalogue and look through all the CVs of everybody that was in it and think, 'we are never going to get a shot at this art world shit', because everyone lived in London, or was from the south.

— As an artist, do you feel like you're part of a movement or a London-based art scene?
I think this current era is about the individuals, rather than a movement. Maybe one day it will be classed as a movement, when it's too late, when I've gone. It's interesting though, talking about where people come from and where they end up. Saying a London-based artist, or an Amsterdam-based artist, or wherever you're based, actually. I mean people use the word 'based' too much because most people just end up somewhere. It's like Richard Wentworth says, 'when you arrive in London, where you spend your first night, that's the area you are most likely to end up living in'. There is a definite truth in that. Then there is the thing about where you're from. I was bitter about everyone being from London, and the art world being 'London-centric'. It's not really that non-representational when you think about it. I don't live full-time in London anymore. I live in Suffolk in a little flat and have this studio here. Anyway, if you are exhibiting internationally then where you are based doesn't really matter as much.

John Russell, from BANK art collective, said a nice thing: 'If you want to sell your pig, you have to take it to the market.' Which is kind of true, isn't it? I mean, imagine being a formula one driver and living on an island that's only a hundred metres long. You would never get your speed up.

— Your work doesn't seem to have a recognizable visual signature either, does it?
I am not known for one. This has pros and cons. I think the con is that no one looks at artwork by me and goes, 'oh, it's a Ryan Gander'. You never really get that well known, or you never really get a popular following of people who go, 'it's a shark, or something in a tank, so it's got to be a Damien Hirst', or, 'it's a bed, or a neon that says fuck – it's got to be Tracey Emin'. You don't get it with me. Most artists have that, don't they? Their own stylistic signature. The pro is – you don't get loads of arseholes as your audience who are only interested in art for something to talk about at dinner parties.

An absolute bereavement of the senses illustrated, 2010 – CREDIT A Burger

I think this current era is about the individuals, rather than a movement. Maybe one day it will be classed as a movement, when it's too late, when I've gone

— So who do you think your audience is then?
I'd hazard a guess: intellectuals, people who are interested in culture, who invest their time and read books, people who don't necessarily want flashy things that are drip-fed to them, and who don't want the same experience as everyone else in the world. I don't know whether that is true, it's just speculation.

— You reference history of art, design and media within your practice. It is sometimes complex to decipher. Would you agree?
Yes, within a strain of my work there is the referencing. This calls for the viewer to be intellectually willing to break down the language. It isn't always immediately obvious. Viewers need to invest some time and energy if they are interested enough to make the connections. I am just interested in the world, in experiences and historical and popular culture with it – X-files and Japanese curry – I think of these things as equally interesting. It's about being able to borrow or use

them for content, and also about recognizing the potential of anything in the world. There is always something left for the viewer, always things left to be discovered – I try for there to be ways in.

— How do you go about research? Books?
It's hard that. I carry a camera, take photos and build upon a collection of thousands of images of things that I see that could... or that will remind me of something that I thought was interesting. This could be the idea of someone walking behind a phone box and reappearing on the other side as another person, or it could be the idea that it would be nice to redesign the Big Mac wrapper, or it could just be an interesting photo of a palm tree on a window. I make notes when I read, just things that interest me. A book by Victor Papanek called *Design for the Real World: Human Ecology and Social Change* from the 70s is brilliant. He is a furniture designer and thinker who used sustainable methods. Or '*The House Of The Future*'; this was a plastic structure

Bauhaus Revisited, 2003 PHOTO CREDIT: The Artist

designed by MIT and Walt Disney's Imagineering group in the 50s. This was the design and development part of the Disney office – the Imagineering office – that's interesting... So I wrote it down. Then all those things are recorded, and maybe a year or two later, when they develop and become more substantial in my head, I type them up and they turn into these ideas [pointing at the numerous pieces of A4 paper with bold black descriptive text, covering large parts of the studio walls] where they are more of a formulated idea as this stage.

I think that if you look at any one of these, you wouldn't imagine what I imagine. That is what is interesting. I have started tweeting them because there are loads. As an exercise, I will give them away so people can respond to them and we can see where it ends up. That will hopefully make me generate new ones. The fact that there are loads of artists who have one idea, and they make it all the time – I thought it would be funny to say you should train your imagination. It is a bit like going on a jogging machine – you get better at running. Imagine if you start 'Imagineering', having ideas. Your imagination gets fast; a quickness I enjoy.

— *How do you tailor the ideas for an exhibition and decide which are successful enough?*
Well, every idea is equally interesting. If I've been concerned enough to point my camera at it, or write it down, then it must be interesting enough. I'll instinctively know that it's not good to have 'silhouettes of thoughts' and 'wow party illustration' together, because they are both drawing-based, but a 'learning game' would probably be a sculptural project – they would go well together in the show because they would collide with each other. I can sort of curate before I make the works. By doing that I can make a show. A solo show that is self-curated.

— *You have talked about self-curating your own shows. What are the differences in curating your own show and curating a group show that may or may not include yourself?*

Maybe self-curating is a different term to curating. I don't think I am a curator: when I have done it, I am not particularly good at it. Possibly that's also because you can't control exactly what's being made. If you make the work for a curated show, then it's going to be an interesting show for you. Some curators do that, these ego curators that are very popular at the moment, who just say to artists, 'I am going to make a work about this theme, can you make a work that illustrates this theme?' – and because they are big curators, the artists go, 'yeah ok', and that's a bit crap, isn't it? I think there is a difference between curating and making a good group show. It doesn't necessarily have to be curated. It can just be a load of good artists put in the same room, who talk to each other all day, who engage with each other.

— *You have just come back from Milan, where you curated the first exhibition for the Lisson Gallery Milan. How was that?*
It was like a big wedding, with limousines and a grand piano in the garden. Imagine a dessert buffet 500 metres long with hundreds of desserts on it... But you're not talking about the party, are you? [Laughs]

— *How did you select the artists for this exhibition, which was titled, 'I know about creative block and I know not to call it by name'?*
There is a situation and context to everything, isn't there? Like dinner the night before last, my mum was coming over. She has a gluten intolerance. Pasta, you can't do it. Narrowed down. My daughter has to eat also, and she is only two and loves corn, baked beans and noodles and that's it. OK, so it has to have one of these ingredients. You know, everything is narrowed down. So the 'narrowing it down' for the exhibition was... To use Lisson artists, they are among the best artists to choose from anyway. Many artists I admire the most are with the gallery, so that's a good starting point. Don't get fussy, or confusing, putting other artists in. It is the opening exhibition, so it has to be a big statement. But what's the Italian art world expecting? Perhaps they are

Porthole to culturefield, 2009, CREDIT Jean Brasille

Parallel Cards – CREDIT John Newton

Imagine being a formula one driver and living on an island that's only a hundred metres long. You would never get your speed up

expecting a show by Anish Kapoor, because that's all they know of Lisson. So you want to give them the exact opposite of that, so you give them a show that's about artists who have practice, and you put all the young guns in it. That was my thinking. I picked the artists first, not the work. Then I thought, 'I am interested in this idea of magic dust, other things that people don't see. Or people being superstitious about their ideas, or about letting their ideas out of the studio – the idea of development and practice being more important than the final thing, so I selected all the works that was in the inventory that were like that, works that were not sold, so they could try and sell them. And really, in the end, I showed my favourite artists and the favourite works I could get my hands on. They all happened to be about this superstition to making.

— *You have been exhibiting extensively of late. How is your schedule? Do you find it hard to push forward new work?*
Travelling is kept to a minimum because of my father. But I have been travelling a lot. Where have I been now? Hum... Berlin, Amsterdam, New York, Milan, Venice for the Biennale, and Japan a few times over the last year or so... A lot of Japan. We will be going there much more over the next few years. It goes through waves, I guess. One Japanese gallery or collector likes your practice, shows your work to their friends, or associates, then they invite you over to do a project, and it escalates from that, there can be a certain amount of trending.

With exhibiting work there is not really a choice. It is just the way it happens. Usually group shows tend to be old works that have previously been shown, and my new works are only for commercial shows and galleries, and then those works get filtered down to museum shows. That's the way it works I think. For Biennials you are meant to produce new work, but I sometimes rework a project that I am working

on, because, at the end of the day, the commercial shows pay the bills, don't they? There would not be any work if the bills were not paid, so you have to give attention to the commercial shows.

There are always other projects I want to realize that cost money and don't make any money. It's like a seesaw. Sometimes you have to do the hardest things, like four commercial shows in a run, but it's okay when they are punctuated by the night school things in the studio, or making a big film, or making a book, or writing a TV script, or doing a cocktail bar, because they are the things that are more interesting and fun.

— *You have always been producing printed material, throughout your career.*
I have worked on twelve publishing projects to date. Two are catalogues, ten are artist's books, and some are works in themselves, part of my artistic practice. I did a touring show three or four years ago, and they wanted an accompanying catalogue of the work in the touring exhibition, so I did that. Otherwise I would have preferred to create an artist's book. The last catalogue titled, *Catalogue Reasonable Vol 1*, that I did in 2010 is an artist's book and catalogue all in one - divided into two halves. It is quite important to have a catalogue when you get enough works, because you forget the titles. It's a good reference to have – shame it's not pocket size.

There have been times when museums say there is money for a book. When I had an exhibition at MUMOK in Vienna, they said there was a budget for a book and I said I didn't want to do a book. Instead, I did *Parallel Cards* – a project in the form of (double fronted) playing cards. They are randomly mixed so you turn one over and it's a king of hearts and you turn it over again and it's the 3 of diamonds... It's two packs verso on verso. Then I invented new games with friends, like Patience in the Mirror. We made them and packaged them with a PO Box address, so if people invented their own games they could send them in and then we would make a book of those games. With the design collective Europa we hosted a cards tournament. Visual art is a game. That is a good use of [the gallery's] money, because you're not just making a book of the work in the show, you're making a completely new work, and I enjoy making new work.

— *That is a very design way of thinking. At this moment in time, do you see yourself as an artist or a designer?*
Neither. As an instigator. It is difficult to really distinguish between the two, as all good artists are designers in a way. They are logical thinkers. The best creatives for me aren't always necessarily artists, they are conceptualists. Like the amazing designer Masamichi Katayama, who founded the interior design firm Wonderwall, in Japan. Or even the musician Pharell Williams from N.E.R.D. He is just like a conceptual artist, but he works in all sorts of different realms, collaborates with all sorts of different people, designs clothes, orchestrates the way people look and the way they sound, writes their music and packages it. It's similar to making conceptual art.

— *You recently collaborated with furniture designer Michael Marriott for the exhibition 'Ernö Goldfinger v Groucho Marx'. How did this come about?*
I am old friends with Marriott, and The Russian Club asked if we would like to work together on something. We have a shared appreciation for the modernist architect Ernö Goldfinger. It was a collaboration on the idea of the show, and it evolved from there… whilst keeping the other person in mind when creating the content. My work 'LAX' is a sculptural rework of my 'Loose Association' lectures in the form of a wooden vitrine similar to Goldfinger's one. Things were kept loose – it translates better for me.

I have this scarf that I am working on at the moment – covered in those perfume samples you pick up in airports. I collected them and wrote the name of the airport and the scent on it. But they are printed onto a big shawl so you can't smell them. It is this big design that could be made and placed in a museum… or I could mass-produce them. It just depends on the context. I believe people think that things only exist within the realms of art when they are charged and highlighted in a gallery or museum. You can see things as astonishing and innovative outside the gallery space – if only you open your eyes.

www.lissongallery.com

APFEL
EVERY
EXTRAORDINARY
DAY

SURPRISE

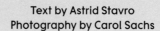

Text by Astrid Stavro
Photography by Carol Sachs

Based in creative, truculent Hackney in East London, APFEL, (A Practice for Every Day Life), routinely draw together stories that translate the ordinary into the extraordinary. This approach has lead to thoughtful and inspired designs, establishing their reputation for intelligent and innovative work. Uniting almost academic research methods with spontaneous, honest, instinctive responses to a variety of subject matter and materials, APFEL are constantly collecting, investigating and experimenting – moving between graphic design, art history, architecture and interior design. 'We are ambitious and committed,' APFEL founders Kirsty Carter and Emma Thomas tell Astrid Stavro. The following interview is ample proof of this.

— *Tell us about your early influences.*
Emma Thomas: I loved drawing and collaging, and made my first 'magazine' when I was ten years old, that I distributed by bike. I worked for an exhibition design firm between the ages of fourteen and eighteen. And I adored David Hockney's work; they had just opened his gallery Salts Mills in Yorkshire, which was only half an hour from where I lived. I decided I wanted to be a graphic artist in London – I thought this was the best way of being able to work with every subject matter and work on paper and architecture.

Kirsty Carter: Very early influences came from my family. My parents are not in the creative industries, but their interest grew when they realized they had a little aspiring artist as their daughter. They took me to museums and galleries from an early age. Then the biggest transformation was my father buying our family Apple Mac computer when I was thirteen years old (this was unusual at the time). Then suddenly I was a graphic designer, doing my homework in ClarisWorks and Photoshop.

— *Where does the name A Practice for Everyday Life come from?*
ET/KC: The name was taken from a book called 'The Practice of Everyday Life' by Michel de Certeau, in which de Certeau describes his way of making sense of the city with eyes open, collecting materials, drawing together stories – we liked the reference to 'practice' as a habit, exercise and pursuit.

— *How and why did you start working together?*
ET/KC: We shared a studio at the Royal College of Art. We also shared a passion for contemporary art. And we discussed our projects together – we started working together in our own work, then tried a couple of freelance jobs. It was nice to see how our ideas and approach could work in another context.

— How many people work in your studio?
ET: To date, six. We are ambitious, but we would never want to get too big that we wouldn't be able to sit around one table (say eight or ten people) so we can discuss projects together and be aware of what each other is working on. In terms of the business world, we will always remain a small business.

— You set up APFEL with no previous work experience. What made you decide to go out on your own?
ET/KC: We couldn't imagine it any other way. We had lots of ideas, and wanted to continue our collaboration and see what we could do. We had nothing to lose, both of us had very little money.

— Can you tell us about the risks you took and what you have learned from mistakes?
ET/KC: Writing a business plan while we were at college helped us structure our thoughts and work out how we might be able to work towards earning a living. We were working from Kirsty's flat and, as we got busier, decided that we needed a studio. We were working really hard on developing studio projects alongside work for other people and businesses. We were nominated for [Creative Review's] 'Creative Futures' and commissioned to do an installation in one of the windows at Selfridges, which was a great venue for developing a project we had started in our final year at college – an 'urban conservatory'. We organised a party for this in front of the window and invited people, businesses, etc., who we thought we would work well with, and we gave them all some of the graphic products we had created as part of the window project. We were invited to meetings and briefings through recommendations from the work we had done, and gradually started to build up more work. We applied for a Princes Trust grant, and the Clerkenwell Green Association grant, and these applications and interviews helped us put some of our attention to working on the business and administrative side of the studio. One of APFEL's first breakthroughs (which led us to work further with

many people within the culture sector) was our long working relationship with the Institute of Contemporary Arts in London. Mistakes... When we first started our studio we didn't receive an email for weeks. We realised that the email address we were giving and mailing from was one character too long!

— Do you work together on every project or do you split work evenly?
KC: We meet regularly to discuss projects and the ideas behind them, often we swap projects around if we need too, when the project needs a bit of each other's skills, or through sheer practicality. As we said, we would stop the growth of APFEL as soon as we were too big to sit around one table to discuss ideas.

— What is your ideal client like?
KC: Enthusiastic, intelligent, 'matter of fact' and driven. Also someone who is like-minded: for each project you work on you invest so much love, emotion and time, you want to be working with someone who is as passionate as you and on the same wavelength.

— Are most of your clients based in the UK?
KC: We have worked and taught abroad a lot. Many of these clients we are still working with, but we have, in the last year, spent a lot more time working with English institutions. The projects we have been working on in the UK, like the Hepworth Wakefield, and 'Postmodernism' at the V&A, are large projects, so they have been quite consuming over the last year. The work process is no different; sometimes it takes as long to get to Wakefield and West London during rush hour as it does to take the Eurostar around Europe.

— How much do you research, and how does it inform your work?
ET/KC: It's on-going... We have always researched our projects in great detail and built this into the studio's time. We have come straight from academia, so these principles are

THE LIFE
AND
OPINIONS
OF
TRISTRAM
SHANDY,
GENTLEMAN

BY LAURENCE STERNE
INTRODUCED BY WILL SELF

The Life and Opinion of Tristram Shandy, Gentleman by Laurence Sterne, published by Visual Editions 2010

House of Voltaire pop-up-shop by Studio Voltaire, designed by 6a architects and APFEL 2010

We would never want to get too big that we wouldn't be able to sit around one table

still entrenched in our studio. For *Tristram Shandy*, for example, we looked at first editions in the British Library, read a lot of material about book and author, Laurence Sterne, and also what was happening at the time the book was written in England. The visual elements in the book aren't just decorative; they are inseparable from the text itself. We worked through the book and highlighted each intervention Sterne made; from the different length dashes and asterisks which usually denote words that he wants to say but can't bring himself to write; to the black page or our new version of the marble page; the significance of noses, lines, blank pages, etc. – all are taking elements of text or typography and subverting them. We wanted to highlight original ideas in the book, which had been lost over time through the numerous editions and reprints – partly through economy/standardization by the bigger publishers, but primarily through a lack of passion for the text. Our ambition was to bring the book back to life again. In a way, we put on Shandy's jacket and breathed life back into the book.

— *Finding the right balance between adding new visual elements while staying faithful to the original spirit of the novel must have been tricky... How close to the original are your interventions?*
ET: You are right; the original didn't use fluorescent ink... We wanted to literally highlight the interventions that have a subtext. Initially we started by setting all the dashes at the same lengths as the original, and making all of them fluorescent orange (the various lengths mean either Shandy is pausing for a length of time, or he is censoring something he is thinking, whether it's too obscene, or deemed inappropriate). This 'highlight' then grew to become the language to encourage the reader to start looking and reading simultaneously, like two stories running hand in hand.

In the original edition, the black page is the point in the text marking the death of one of the characters, Yorick, and is a page printed with a black litho plate and no text. At this point, we considered the object of the printing plate and the colour black as an accumulation of printed matter and colours – an end point essentially, which cannot be undone. We took all the text pages leading up to this point in the story – and overprinted them – basically an accumulation of his life to the point when he dies, Yorick's end point.

Our edition celebrates '*The Life and Opinions of Tristram Shandy*' as the first graphic novel, and brings the spirit of the original back to life. Throughout the book, Shandy is obsessed with publishing and the production of 'this book that you are reading', and even writes about going to the printing press obsessing that everything was just right, so it seemed key that (like the original) all our interventions would only use the medium of the traditional book, typography, symbols, line, figures, paper, plates... This draws at-

tention to the self-reflection and consciousness of writing – in a sense Shandy is the first fly-on-the-wall documentary.

— *There seems to be a resurgence of 'hybrid novels', partly embodied by Visual Editions.*
ET: I think what Visual Editions are doing is particular, in that their starting point was looking at novels and thinking, why shouldn't they have the same love and thought put into the design, as, say, an art book, but then make them available to the same market. Many mass-produced novels reached a very ugly and soulless point. What they are posing is opposite to books on Kindle, where the book as object is lost. Having said that, a digital Visual Editions book would be a really interesting brief. There are a lot of very interesting publishers around right now, and a resurgence in successful small independents: Hyphen, Occasional Papers, Ditto, Hato, as well as Book Works, Four Corners, JRP Ringier, all of whom are passionate about the form of the book.

— *Do you think the role of the editorial designer is changing?*
ET: Many of these publishing businesses have been set up by designers and makers who have worked as editorial designers and who see the possibilities for specialized editorial or for going against marketing conventions. They are interested in a more involved approach to design, which is great. It's also going to be interesting to consider editorial print and screen – each has its own charms and uses.

— *Is this the end of print, the survival of the fittest?*
ET: Not an end of print, but more specialized print, perhaps – all the general, reporting, 'fast text' is moving online. Print-on-demand can allow for more self-authorship, more voices, more information and many people want automated or template design, which is an interesting medium to consider. But with more and more materials, information and voices, the role of editors and designers becomes much more important. I don't see fewer books around now, I only see more, and many of them are very well designed.

— *APFEL is known for 'pushing the boundaries of minimalism' – what does this mean to you and how does it reflect in your work?*
ET/KC: We challenge each other, and the studio, to be direct and straightforward. If an idea can be presented minimally, then it can be very beautiful – why would you want to add something else to it?

— *How would you define your work and the thought process behind it?*
ET: We draw together stories that can translate the ordinary into the extraordinary. And it is important to produce unique designs that are for the project, not for us. How can any one

de Certeau describes his way
of making sense of the city
with eyes open, collecting materials,
drawing together stories

project ever look like the other when you put careful thought into understanding what the project needs?

— *Where does your attraction to the odd and the quirky come from?*
KC: People, human beings, are funny; we are all particular individuals made up of very unique parts. We are voyeurs of people's habits, rituals or hobbies – people have such amazing talents, which we like to draw upon in our work.

ET: Maybe this comes from collecting, archiving – processes which are forgotten about, odd things that stand out as being distinctive or might have been forgotten about, things that appear a little strange and make you ask questions. We like to show each other things that make us smile.

— *One of your longest relationships has been with the ICA. How did this productive relationship come about?*
ET/KC: In 2004 we met the then director of exhibitions at a private view. We didn't realize who he was, and he asked us what we thought of the design of the graphics in the new show. We gave it our honest critique and told him it was illegible: there were large paragraphs of text, all in capital letters – basic stuff really. Then he told us he had designed it! He called us in for a meeting the next week. Our working relationship began in 2004, working on 'Becks Futures 2005'. We then went on to work on fourteen different exhibitions. The creative work included the invitation, poster, publication, signage and exhibition design. This kind of long, on-going collaboration with a curator not only got us noticed and allowed us to work on many projects with really great artists, but also illustrated how we could work with an individual and an institution on a level of complete trust; this is something you can only develop over time with a client.

— *You have collaborated with Anthony Burrill, among others. How do these collaborations come about?*
ET/KC: We like each other's work. Initially, Anthony asked us to work with him on some children's games for the Tate, then with FAT architects for the Museum of Croydon. We had a lot of fun, and it brought about a change of dynamic which was interesting. Anthony is our graphic design dad, we did many collaborations together as APFEL|AB and will continue to do so, though we have had a break of a few years. Anthony was fundamental to us at the beginning; he was so full of encouragement and always got us involved in some shape or form. He sends us music every Friday, a 'Friday Banger' to get us through the last part of the week.

— *Is process more important than the end result?*
ET/KC: Without a good working process, the end result is disappointing.

— *Do you work on personal projects?*
KC: A lot of our personal projects link back to our studio work in some way – we put so much of ourselves into our work. For example, we printed and designed a poster based on the front cover we designed for *Tristram Shandy*. We fell in love with the cover (it was full of noses), but for various reasons it wasn't appropriate. Instead of it remaining in a digital file on a hard drive, we persuaded our local printer to print it for free for us and give some copies to Visual Editions to help support them. We also had a pile ourselves to sell. Another example is some new elastic bands we will be launching shortly. They have crazy Sottsass patterns printed on them; we are using them in the Postmodernism exhibition to hold our labels up. We didn't need them mass-produced, but again, we fell in love with them so much, we are going to produce them ourselves. Other projects remain private, and still others are completely unrelated.

— *Are you where you would like to be?*
ET/KC: We love working with print, and we would like to continue this as well as develop more multidisciplinary projects in the studio. Recently, we collaborated on an animation with Arvid Niklasson, for Adam Broomberg and Oliver Chanarin's video for Massive Attack – it was great to work with moving images again, and we would be very happy do more. We would also jump at the challenge of designing a space or pattern of rituals for a restaurant or shop, and designing textiles or collaborating with a fashion designer. We are very open to all kinds of projects and look to grow in many different ways, again as Mr Thomas said... anything can be possible when you put your mind to it.

www.apracticeforeverydaylife.com

Postmodernism: Style and Subversion 1970–1990 by Victoria and Albert Museum, designed by Carmody Groarke and APFEL 2011

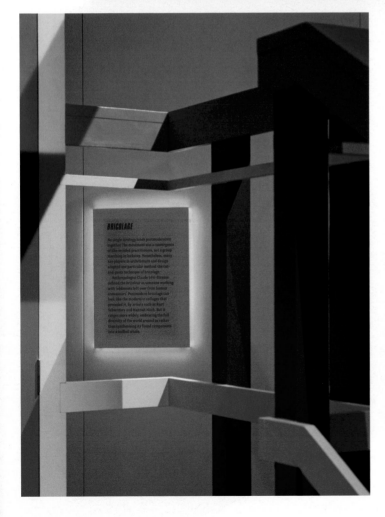

Las Vegas — the strip
1966

Photographs by Robert Venturi
and Denise Scott Brown
Courtesy of Venturi, Scott Brown
and Associates, Inc., Philadelphia

Viktor Timofeev

REDBLACK / Cyclical Nature (detail), 2007-2011, gouache, watercolor on paper, 24.1 x 33 cm, in 48 parts

Text by Natasha Hoare
Photography by Anja Schaffner

WORLD MAKING

Viktor Timofeev is an artist whose paintings are gaining him considerable international attention. Championed by gallerist wunderkind Hannah Barry, and exhibiting internationally in Germany, Austria and the US, Timofeev's is a star on the rise. Latvian born, he moved to the US as a youngster to live in the architectural splendour of New York. Splitting his time between skating, playing in bands and video games, he was later diagnosed with a chronic foot problem, leaving him unable to skateboard; something on which he had based his whole life. Wanting to keep travelling to Manhattan's skate spots with his crew, he began to sit and draw the buildings that dwarfed them. What started with doodles soon grew into a passion for art, prompting him to switch from his computer science course in college to art history and practice.

Prolific and intense, Timofeev works across many different media in order to arrive at his paintings. His studio walls are covered with drawings, a process central to the formation of his compositions on canvas, and shelves hold ranks of strange geometric constructions or maquettes, through which he explores the forms that populate his paintings. The room has a strange effect, like introducing one to the inside of his mind, and feels like an attempt to keep those thoughts, which whirl around his skull at a hundred mph, in check. The nearby skate park provides an essential exorcism for the energy that accrues during his time in the studio.

He has a magpie mind, picking up thousands of references and ideas, which relate to manufactured spaces and the utopian artistic impulses behind them. His knowledge of these is truly diverse, drawing inspiration from everything: from Renaissance architecture to Buckminster Fuller, the PC game Doom to Surrealist painters. His love of architecture is illuminating; in his paintings one has a profound sense that he is above all acting as an architect of pictorial space.

His vertiginous canvases are large in scale and plunge the viewer into a pixelated world of hulking mechanical creatures moving through latticed spaces of repeated mathematical forms, animated by a restricted palette of colours. These worlds recede infinitesimally into the distance, creating dizzying perspectival vortexes some would find terrifying, but which he finds alluringly comforting and tragically out of reach.

The digital process of optimisation is a fitting concern for Timofeev, whose own work is developing in style and technique around issues of control and expression. Through his early work he has been building up a tight conceptual structure and technical ability, evidenced by a year long drawing project in 2007, which he undertook in order to understand the difference between looking and seeing. He now breaks these systems down to serve more expressive purposes, and as such, has reached an exciting moment in the development of his art.

Viktor Timofeev

The more our lives get transferred into bits and bytes, the more we will come to re-appreciate the analogue

— Could you tell us a bit about how your background and how it relates to you what you are doing now?

I got a box of crayons as a gift in kindergarten, but they were all various shades of grey. The obsession with drawing probably started then. My parents were supportive early on – my dad showed me how to make isometric drawings of cars back in Riga. He also showed me a pencil portrait he did of my mom. It's still etched in my memory. I used to draw a comic strip about the adventures of Patat, a wedge-shaped handful of fried potatoes.

— You were born in Latvia and studied in New York before moving to Berlin, what brought you to Germany?

I moved to Berlin three years ago, via London. I was due to study at the RCA [Royal College of Art] in London, but we had a dispute over tuition fees that we couldn't resolve in time. I just needed to keep working, especially as I had just reached a pivotal moment with my last painting completed in New York (*Rubik's Houses*, 2008). Berlin allowed me the time and space to do just that, and I'm still stuck here.

— How was this painting a huge turning point for you?

Everything that I was interested in combined together. It just felt like it was this really big moment. Chromatic codes, the twisted archetype, the cold landscape, rendered space - it was all there. I was still painting in a flat, precise way, but it was still all there.

— Have you always skated?

I've been skating for more than half of my life at this point. In college I was diagnosed with a condition in my feet that was supposed to be chronic. It was a real identity shock, as skating was woven into every part of my being. So, at first, I still used to go to skate spots with my friends, and I started to draw there. I just drew buildings in Manhattan and even some skate obstacles, just normal late-teen doodles. Then I switched my course of study, from computer science to art history and art. The withdrawal from the skate world was heavy, but it also gave me space to absorb other things, like art. I'm lucky to be able to push around and skate now, though I'm careful not to bring it too close to my heart...

192.128.13.15 [RESIDUAL DIVIDUAL], 2011, ink on paper, 37.5cm x 55cm

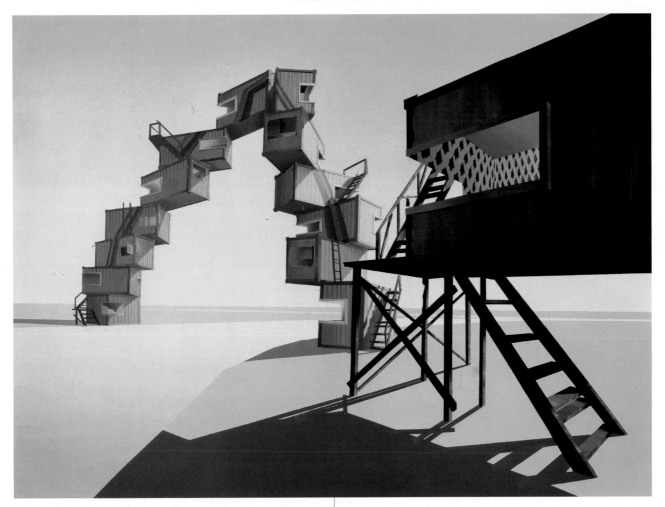

LPZG_84 enamel (detail), 2009, acrylic on canvas. 150cm x 195cm

— *You work on large-scale canvases, which are often highly detailed in their geometric composition and intricate colour schemes. How long do you spend in front of each?*
I try not to spend more than a week on a single work. Because I can spend way too much time on it and end up suffocating it. The work can become too precious, and you worry if your next layer will kill the whole thing. You should always just try it.

— *On your blog you have images by Rene Magritte and Yves Tanguy; is surrealist work an influence on you?*
With Magritte particularly, it's his peculiar juxtapositions of carefully selected objects and the atmospheric dead stillness, like a video grab of a data mash-up video re-translated into really lucid pictorial logic. I like Tanguy's invention of systems, of logic and hierarchy. It's like he is making a picture of things he found on Mars, and that, even there, he has declared that inequalities exist – parasites and hosts. I've been more influenced by this kind of work – setting up an autonomous system and then either upsetting it, or reinforcing it, over and over.

— *The surrealists had a profound relationship with the unconscious and dreams. Does your work touch on these also?*
I think of dreams as mediated by our relationships and experiences with recognizable objects and forms from the environment, as opposed to the invisible abstract language that is defining our lives more and more. With things like geofencing and 'gamification', we are transferring every part of our lives into an augmented reality with metaphysical parameters. Since this tertiary reality is more real to us than our primary physical reality, our dreams are probably also now mediated by it. We dream in Facebook. I kind of see my work starting there.

— *Your work is informed by computer game graphics and animations, and I have read your essay on Doom and the archaeology of computer games. As a child, did you play many of them? How do they inform your work?*
PC games like Wolfenstein 3D and Doom form some of my earliest memories of digital space, which is interesting since they are already evolved from the early console two-dimensional platforms, such as Mario Bros. They take me back to a specific time and place, when I was on different terms with my environment, still adjusting to both physical and digital reality. I played Wolfenstein with my dad, back in Riga from an early age: it was like our bonding thing. I've really only started to think about the relationship between game-worlds and my work in the past few years, as I got more and more attracted to fantasy utopias and perfect cities where the air tastes like sugar. These virtual utopias are expressions of what we collectively desire. Revisiting a lot of these game-spaces, I go through them much slower than initially, savouring the digital déja-vu and just spending time there, remembering my first encounters. This kind of archaeology is probably more of a personal journey than anything, but it makes me think about the future of optimization and where we're headed.

A line that wavers can communicate something very different. Morandi's still lives are so visceral, so alive because of his immense attention to line

— What attracts you to these fabricated worlds?
I was really easily seduced by the vocabulary of the Constructivists in Russia, circa 1918. But that led me into other things like Buckminster Fuller and then backwards to William Morris. History is so fluid and non-linear now that time doesn't exist thanks to the Internet! Anyway, I'm really drawn to working within parameters and using generators. In school I fell in love with Renaissance architecture, which I saw as a perpetual quest for a perfected vocabulary of fabrication. There was a strong belief that by utilizing the correct proportions, architecture will click with the universal order and change society. But what happened when it was perfected? Well, it sort of eliminated the individual's imagination and became only a three dimensional manifestation of order. All of a sudden unresolved, goofy-looking façade problems became much more interesting. So the Mannerists took these canonical systems and skewed and exaggerated them, played games with the vocabulary. I do the same thing with my generators and parameters – set them up and then push them further, creating ambiguities, contradictions and redundancies; what I see as the real content.

— Is your work inspired by the communist utopias?
I have definitely spent a fair amount of time studying the architectural drawings of the Socialist Revolution. It is such an amazing pocket of history. I wouldn't say that it particularly influences my work more than any other communal utopias though. So much of the communist vocabulary is problematic in retrospect – we have learned that glass and steel can satisfy a capitalist society as well as a communist one, if not better.

— Despite quoting the online world, you work in the traditional media of painting, drawing and sculpture. Do you ever program your own games and spaces?
At this point, I'm only interested in the logic underneath code. I don't want to spend any more time in front of a computer than I have to, because the more our lives get transferred into bits and bytes, the more we will come to re-appreciate the analogue – asking what it means to draw or paint in 2011 is more relevant than ever. There is this meta-narrative that I always think about framing my work – remembering a world that was built only on memories of its digital mimesis, machine hyper-rationality as only a starting point; I guess it's what happens when you grow up with id software as your babysitter.

— When did you actually start drawing?
I switched my major six times while in school. I started in computer science and ended up in art. I was really into life drawing classes. I was obsessed with Ingres, roman statues, cross-hatching, Fabriano paper… After drawing nudes I would go outside and draw buildings the rest of the day. I started to treat buildings like characters, and the streets like pedestals.

— Do you carry a sketchbook or a camera?
These days I carry a camera and two pocket-sized books, which I use just for ideas and doodles. Once I get back to studio, I copy the doodles to a larger doodle book that stays in the studio. I take photos of interesting things I see on the street, print them out and put them on my wall in order to slowly absorb them.

— Do you draw from life, or from photographs?
I never work from photographs. With the way my work has developed it simply doesn't make sense. What I am involved with is invention, not replication. I make a lot of three-dimensional models if I want to wrap my mind around a complex form and then do some life drawings from that just to study it. Working directly from photographs can result in some seriously boring work and it is a slippery slope to complete reliance on the medium. It doesn't train your eyes to see – only to look.

— Do you see drawing as a tool and a means to an end, or as an end in itself?
Drawing is both an end in itself and integral to everything I do. I would not be able to make the paintings that I make had I not been seriously involved with purely drawing for a number of years beforehand. I think every medium has its own language and methods; they can inform each other and help push each other's limits, but ultimately work on different levels. Compare the line quality of Morandi's etchings to his paintings.

— Do you work from a studio?
When I first started drawing seriously, I worked outside, drawing buildings and streets. Now I only work in the studio, with my maquettes, sketches, books of patterns all around. I need a certain amount of clarity, peace and order when working, so a studio is simply necessary. I can also listen to talk radio all day while working, though I do have to switch off the Internet to really focus.

I like to think of it as world making. My world isn't necessarily parallel, as that implies they never meet. I would say my world meanders around our reality

— *Do you do something to warm up?*
I usually make several preparatory, compositional studies for anything I make, from a small ink drawing to a huge painting. But generally the best thing to do is just dive in; the quicker you make mistakes the quicker you can attempt to resolve them.

— *The title of your show at the Hannah Barry Gallery in London is* MONSTROcity; *is this a mythical city of your creation?*
The first show at Hannah Barry Gallery surrounded a local area network – a generic community of nodes, just like any office. Now I am starting to break it down into hierarchies. Imagine a map of the network – the relative East and West will generate their own behaviour because this human condition feeds into everything. This desire to create, to be different, is embedded in all of us. *MONSTROcity* is the first chapter, and is a place full of optimism. The constant skewing, stacking and rebuilding of parameters suggests that we are never really happy with what we have, and we keep going, which I see as beautiful. It's tragic as well, as this utopian destination can never physically exist.

— *You have a very art historical approach to the construction of space, using the rules of perspective to create sublime volumes and spaces within the flat pane of the canvas. Your recent paintings for* MONSTROcity *break down the accuracy of your line and the geometry of your subjects. Why has this started to happen?*
From control comes freedom – before I couldn't allow myself to be so indulgent. I wanted to build a foundation out of stones, and so they needed to be solid. That's why I did this yearlong drawing project in 2007; to understand the difference between looking and seeing. I made lines straight by default in order to limit the variables involved. Slowly, I became more comfortable with exposing my meandering marks, and accepted my history with cartoons and doodles. A line that wavers can communicate something very different. Morandi's still lifes are so visceral, so alive because of his immense attention to line!

— *Your palette has changes also.*
Yeah, it's the same though. I still organize everything around the primary colours, black and white. The tight parameters have started to expand a bit – modulating saturation, for example.

— *Your Soundcloud account is an amazing sonic landscape that seems to directly correlate to the unfolding spaces of your paintings. What role does music play in your practice?*
Only recently have I been comfortable sharing my music alongside my artwork. My first LP, *GIVE HEALTH999*, comes from a similar place and deals with similar issues – the sublime nature of digital space, being aware that something is a simulation but falling in love with it anyway. It's all constructed from analogue instruments, generated through digital filters. Striving to be a machine, but failing and finding solace in that melancholy.

— *What are you working on next?*
I'm working on a show for the Kunsthalle Exnergasse in Vienna called *You Are Free*, with a group of friends from Berlin and New York. The show is about the link between the utopian impulse of music making and art making, so I will be playing some music there as well.

— *How would you define what it is that you do?*
I like to think of it as world making. My world isn't necessarily parallel, as that implies they never meet. I would say my world meanders around our reality, appropriating a certain vocabulary while completely inventing another. I suppose it can be seen as a hybrid in that sense. The constructions and characters that inhabit this world are the content of my work, and it is through them that I program meaning and narrative.

www.victortimofeev.com
www.hannahbarry.com

REDBLACK / Cyclical Nature, 2007-2011, gouache, watercolor on paper, 24.1 x 33 cm, in 48 parts

IV

Chris Burden

Shoot, November 19 1971, F Space, Santa Ana, CA

Text by Katya Tylevich
Photography by Alexei Tylevich

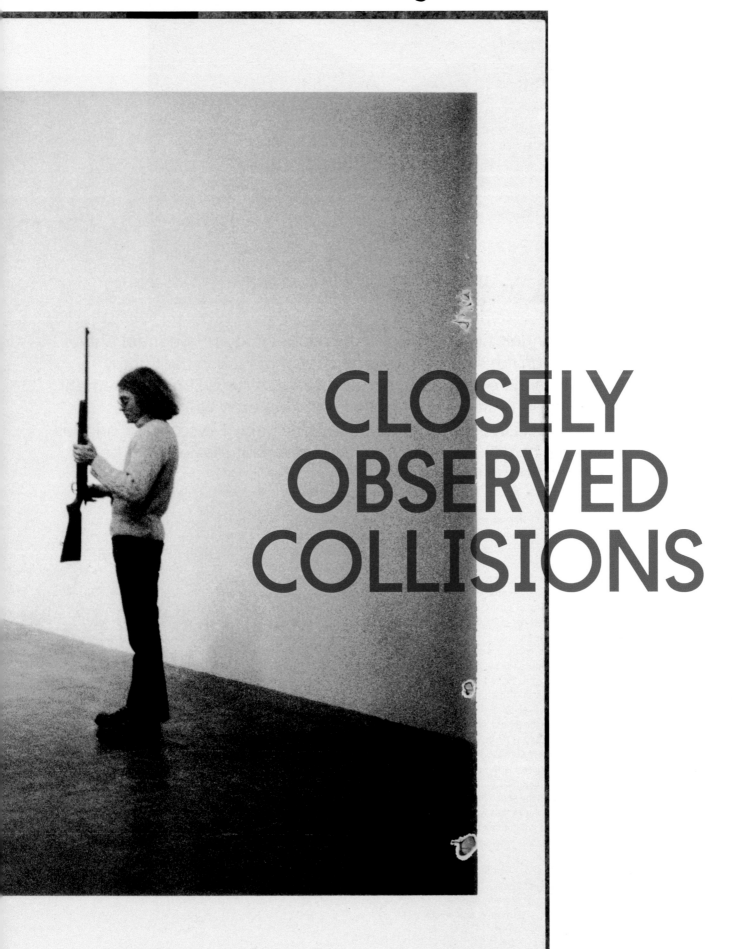

CLOSELY
OBSERVED
COLLISIONS

Worlds away from Los Angeles (some 50 km north of downtown), we meet Chris Burden in his Topanga Canyon studio, on a large stretch of land in the Santa Monica Mountains. Given the geography, 'secluded' should be an understatement for the property, but Burden's studio feels quite inhabited, busy with people working on various projects in every corner of the workspace. Skyscrapers, bridges. At one point, he tells me he'd like to build a railroad here, but the Zeppelin he wants to make — to fly around the canyons — might take priority.

Burden saves me the trouble of starting a conversation; we shake hands and he immediately launches into descriptions of his works-in-progress, walking excitedly from one room to the other and speaking quickly, offering few obvious breaks for my questions. Mostly, he speaks of engineering feats and meticulous experimentations. He's not opening his heart up about the meaning of getting shot in the arm, here, ladies and gentleman. It's not going to be that kind of conversation. Still, I can't help but hear what he's not saying — whether or not I hear correctly is a question still to be answered. Several times I venture to say, 'oh, so this means that,' only to have Burden tell me, 'no it doesn't.'

For the record, I didn't go into this meeting expecting Chris Burden to be a black and white, two-dimensional version of himself, bleeding from the palms, crucified to a Volkswagen Beetle [*Trans-fixed*, 1974] — but I'm only human. I've read things, seen pictures. I admit to carrying some art history baggage. After all, Burden is in the Zeus league of art mythology, owing in no small part to his 1970s performance artworks, ephemeral in the sense that they can never really be recreated, but undying in that way explosive moments are undying, especially when documented just-so by evocative photographs that make their way into collective memory (and now the Internet).

I'd like to avoid speaking about Burden's work as if it's separated by the past and present tense; there is no necessary break between the black and white photographs and the ones in colour, between 'performative' and 'sculptural,' and 'architectural,' for example. Personally, I can't help but hear a similar whisper in most of Burden's works: 'Look, it's a beautiful landmine. Don't step on it.' Burden's project *Samson* [1985], for example – which has every visitor of a museum passing through a turnstile that is connected to a gearbox and a 100 ton jack. Every time a visitor enters, the jack is expanded, adding to the pressure against the walls — which could theoretically push the walls down. Or take *The Flying Steamroller* [1996], a sculpture made of a 12-ton steamroller, attached to a pivoting arm; at maximum speed, the steamroller revolves, lifting off the ground, as if flying. But we'll get to the word 'scary' (and, in the same breath, 'exhilarating') when we talk about the falling beams, and skyscrapers, later. First, I'd like to linger on the word 'tempting'.

In his energetic tour of the studio, Chris Burden enters the central room and motions to a table covered in glass parts. This piece [*Large Glass Ship*, 1983] went to a show in Barcelona in 1995, and they dropped the whole container on the way back. It belongs to the Orange County Museum of Art. We spent years writing letters, but the museum in Barcelona wouldn't take responsibility for it, and now the museum down in Orange County decided to file an insurance claim. So we're trying to make another one for them. That's our restoration or 're-making' project. But there's no way we can match the original. It doesn't have to be perfect, though. We just need the spirit of it.

Chris Burden

*Hell Gate, 1998, Metal toy construction parts (Meccano and Erector), and wood
225 x 861 x 102 cm*

I open my mouth, ask a question about the spirit of a 're-make,' but we'll have to get back to that later. Burden's attention is already on another piece — a bridge — in the middle of the studio.
This is called the *21 Foot Truss Bridge* [2002]. It's so light you can pick it up. I make the parts myself now, out of stainless steel, but they're copies of original American Meccano from 1913. I did use original Meccano in some of the bridges, like *Hell Gate Bridge* [1998, one of Burden's first bridges], which has parts first made in 1913. But regular steel rusts, and the more Meccano I bought, the more expensive it became, because I was buying up the world's supply. I thought: this is crazy! Now, we use stainless steel. We did a skyscraper in New York City at Rockefeller Plaza [*What My Dad Gave Me*, 2008]: sixty-five feet high, this thing. It was a million parts. It was huge.

Without catching breath, Burden leads us into another room, where a new steel tower is on its side; people are working on it.
You'll be able to walk up this one, using a ladder. But I don't really want people to climb this. Do you know what I'm saying? I want it to be physically possible, but not something I want the public to actually do. All it takes is one young drunk...

— But you've created the temptation. Is it forbidden fruit?
It's not about trying to participate in the work: it's that you see the structure and the material that it's made of. It's thin metal, that's all. We've just braced it in every direction and all of a sudden, it's extremely strong.

— So what's to stop someone from walking on this structure?
We'll have something. It would also depend on the situation... is it in somebody's backyard, or in a shopping mall in Vienna?

— Where would you like to see it, ideally?
I made it as part of a series of towers I'm doing for a new city called Xanadu — a city that nobody lives in. It was a proposal I did for L.A. County Art Museum, but I'm not sure it's going to happen because of finances. It could go someplace else. I have the idea of maybe putting some of these up at Larry Gagosian's home in Beverly Hills. [Looking back to the tower on its side.] This looks like child's play. And the basis for it is a toy. But it's not child's play. You really have to be careful. You have to concentrate because this joint is different from that joint. They're all different, so if you make a mistake in there... [Laughs.]

— How much control do you feel you have over your work, once its 'out there'?
Even the best engineering can fail. Think of the Airbus with the engine that blows up, right? What happened guys? Well, an oil pipe was machined a little off canter. That was a super high-tech thing, but it went wrong, for whatever reason. So, I mean, how much control can you really have over something like *Beam Drop*? [*Beam Drop New York*, 1984 / *Beam Drop Inhotim*, 2008 / *Beam Drop Antwerp*, 2009; sculptures created by dropping large steal beams from a crane into wet cement below.] Not much, once you let go of the beam. You lower it close to where you hope it'll land, but at some point you have to let it drop. And if one of those beams hits you, you don't go to the hospital, you go to the morgue.

[I laugh.]

I'm serious. In Antwerp we had some really heavy beams they tried to lift up, and they could only get them so far off the ground before they released them. Everyone just ran for their lives. It's scary. It's powerful stuff. But that's what makes it exhilarating. People like watching because they've never seen anything like it before. I mean, watching two trains or two airplanes collide — that's really fun, but it's a little dangerous, too.

— Almost every project we've discussed so far has an element of danger to it.

It's how you deal with it. [Changing the subject, Burden flips through a portfolio of project proposals.] This is one I've been working on for a long time: a model Zeppelin, that goes around a model of the Eiffel tower. This Zeppelin will be tethered to the tower, so it won't be able to fly away. I got a machinist to make the motor for me. He tested it over the years, very slowly, every single part. That's important for me. I like the idea that we're building this thing from scratch. This motor's cost me tens of thousands of dollars, which is nuts because, really, you can go down and buy a Honda motor off a motorbike for 150 dollars or something. But that's not what I wanted to do. There's a beauty in making this Zeppelin from scratch. Ideally, we'd even cast our own metal.

Ultimately, this is a sculpture, a memorial — it's like the guy with a sword on a horse. It's memorializing that moment when Alberto Santos-Dumont flew his Zeppelin around the Eiffel Tower in 1901. That was a big deal. It was a big day. In the back of my mind, this piece is about me being able to do what he did. I want to relive that. I would love to actually make a Zeppelin or even a balloon that I could float around in, over the canyons on a calm day. That would be fantastic. The parts are perfectly legal. It's just that the Zeppelin may be illegal. But I don't know what the laws are and I don't think I'll bother to find out. I can tell you now that the police sheriff helicopter will come by and say, 'Land that thing now; we're sending over three squad cars.' Okay, well, I'll only take it out on foggy days when you guys can't catch me.

When you recreate somebody else's performance, it becomes theatre, and that has nothing to do with performance the way I conceived of it in the '70s

What My Dad Gave Me, 2008, Approximately 1,000,000 stainless steel Mysto Type I Erector parts, nuts and bolts, and stainless steel base plate. Skyscraper: 1,981.2 x 341.4 x 341.4 cm, Base: 15.24 x 341.4 x 344.4 cm tubular steel cover with stainless steel veneer. Plinth: Reinforced concrete, 91.4 cm high.

Beam Drop, 1984, Approximately 60 steel I-beams, concrete, Footprint approximately 1066.8 x 1066.8 cm, Installation at Artpark, Lewiston, New York, 8/2/1984. Dismantled May, 1987.

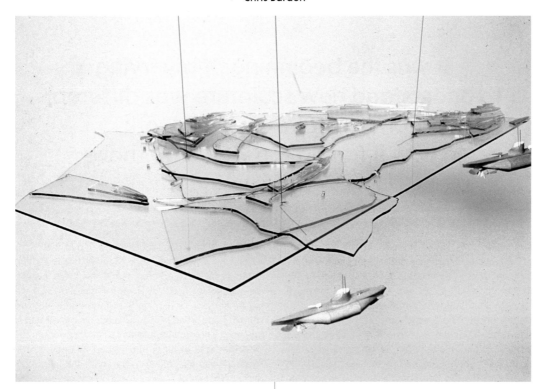

Large Glass Ship, 1983, 0.6 cm plate glass, lead toy soldiers, 4 Lucky Subs (cardboard, Duco cement, wire, Each sub: 7 x 21 x 4.5 cm) 7 x 129.5 x 99 cm

— *Were you always quite conscious of the legal boundaries of your work?*
Oh, God. Yeah, in a certain sense. I mean certainly the performances, but even outdoor pieces that I did in college: it was all about getting permission, moving through the bureaucracy of a college to use the soccer field. I mean, I'd like to show *Xanadu* at Larry Gagosian's house, but he may not want to get into that with his neighbours, you know. He may not want to pay off a city council member with a big envelope. [Laughs.]

But I remember my first show, which I had in graduate school in 1971, with Bruce Nauman and Mowry Baden in La Jolla [California]. Five or six of my apparatus pieces were installed, and they had attendants helping old people use them. It was so crazy! That would never happen in this day and age because of lawsuits and liability issues over people getting hurt. But back then you'd see, you know, a 75 year-old woman trying to get into one of these apparatuses and some gallery attendant assisting her. Even then, I knew that was kind of dangerous. There was always that possibility of someone getting hurt — but I'm not into hurting the viewers. That's not it at all, no. I mean, that tower we're building in the other room: I want to climb it. And I do. But if it's out on the lawn at LACMA [Los Angeles County Museum of Art] and anybody can climb it? No. I don't think so. [Laughs.] That's just asking... I was scared that when [*What My Dad Gave Me*] showed in New York, people would try to climb it.

— *Well, did anyone?*
They had 24-hour security and two cops there. They had video cameras everywhere.

— *Again, we come back to the temptation of danger in your work.*
But I really don't want anybody climbing it — for one thing, that would destroy the structure. It would end it all. I mean, it would be a huge job to fix it. The other thing is, something

can suggest function, without being functional. I mean, a lot of people say to me: 'You've got all of these toy bridges, are you ever going to build a real bridge?' Well, these are real bridges. You just can't walk on them.

— *Do you think of your works as experiments?*
Yes.

— *Is part of the experiment, then, seeing how people react to your projects?*
I don't know how to answer that question. Sometimes. A lot of things don't happen as planned... Like that gold sculpture at Gagosian didn't happen. [Referring to *One Ton; One Kilo*, a show scheduled for the Gagosian Gallery in Beverly Hills in 2009.] I bought a one-ton crane truck that had been used for laying pipe in the Central Valley of California, and I made a one-ton block. It actually does weigh exactly one ton. It's so bizarre, just right on the money: bingo. So the idea was, you walk into the gallery and you see this truck with a one-ton block. So okay: one ton. Where's the one kilo? It sounds like a drug deal, right? But then you go upstairs, where you are expecting to see one kilo — instead, you see not one kilo, but 100 kilos. Just this pile of gold upstairs!

I don't know if you heard about this, but the Gagosian bought the gold — wire transferred 3 million 345 thousand dollars. They'd used a company called Stanford Coin and Bullion. Well, Stanford — anything associated with his name got a yellow piece of tape around it. He was a baby Madoff, right? He embezzled 10 billion. So, because the gold was bought through a subsidiary of that company, the people who were supposed to be holding the gold in Texas said they couldn't release it, even though it was paid for in full. Take a ticket and get in line with the other 30,000 litigants. So they stole the gold! It's so weird.

And everyone had been really worried because: oh, if you show this much gold in Beverly Hills, you're asking for the robbers to come from North Hollywood — the Russians

It was the beginning of my trying to understand how sculpture was different from two-dimensional work in how it forced the viewer to move

with their machine guns, right? They had alarms and a special case; the Beverly Hills police had a direct line. But the gold was stolen before it even got to us! It was stolen by the guys with the coat and ties on, you know what I mean? It was this beautiful metaphor for the financial world.

I was really upset. There was no press for the show: it was all about that moment of surprise. It sounds like there's heroin upstairs, but no, it's gold. So, to answer your question: yeah, that was about people's reactions to the surprise of going upstairs. It's too bad about this project because whoever would have bought it, could have made money just on the value of the bullion. Forget the artwork. Oh, God. But that moment of surprise? I can never recreate that.

— *Other than* Large Glass Ship, *what other works have you recreated?*
With my approval, Pomona College remade an undergraduate work of mine [*Untitled* sculpture, 1967] and installed it in front of the art building. I thought it was kind of nice. The original was Minimalist, really well finished, except that it was made of plywood. So, about a month after I finished it, the finished surface started to crack. I really didn't know what I was doing, then. So they remade the new one out of aluminium with automotive paint. It was an important sculpture for me because it was the beginning of my trying to understand how sculpture was different from two-dimensional work in how it forced the viewer to move. You can't understand this thing physically, if you just stand in one spot. You really have to walk around it to understand that it's trying to trick you. So [the sculpture at Pomona] looks like three columns and, at some points, it looks like two columns. It was a real catalyst for me, when I first made it: I began to understand that just physical activity could be art. You didn't have to have an object. Just doing something could be art. And so it became the basis for performance works that I did years later.

— *These works in your studio now — the bridges, the skyscrapers — do they draw from that same 'breakthrough'?*
Yes, because in order to understand this bridge, you need to walk to either end of it. If you just look at it from one spot, you don't really understand it at all. Sculpture is sort of regarded as the stepchild of the two-dimensional. Two-dimensional work is seen as more intellectual, because it's an illusionary plane. Whereas sculpture — even though it's having a renaissance now — in general, you look at art history, and it's always a second cousin because it's too close to clay, it's too close to the earth, and so it becomes suspect.

— *Whoa. Where does architecture fit into that?*
I won't go down that road. Architecture is a different ball game, really. It's a different hierarchy. When I was doing the installation for LACMA [*Urban Light*, 2008], I was treading on some very thin ice with the people who worked for Renzo Piano when I said: 'This building is here to house the fine arts. The architecture has to accommodate the art, not the other way around, and I need X amount of room between my lamps. I'm sorry, but that's the hierarchy.'

— *Judging by your work, surely you've dealt with architects before. [i.e.* Wexner Castle, *1990, in which Burden added crenels and merlons to a Peter Eisenman-designed museum.]*
I knew what the deal was. Piano had the idea of creating a void between the new building and the old building — that would be the breathing spot, the white page in the catalogue — and then I wanted to fill it up with lamps that looked kind of architectural, and had a peaked roof. That was not his idea of the plaza. He had the European vision that a plaza was supposed to be empty so that people would gather there. Of course, in L.A., nobody would gather in an empty plaza. It's L.A. It's only because the lamps are there that people gather. So, now the lamps really are an architecture, in a way. They're like a Parthenon without a roof, and a destination point. In my wildest imagination, I didn't realize they would become so popular. But you realize L.A. doesn't have many icons: There's the Hollywood sign. There's Grauman's Chinese Theatre in Hollywood. Disneyland? The beach?

— *How much did architecture figure into your earlier performance work?*
Architecture is what inspired a lot of it. It was all about response to an architectural situation — *Doorway to Heaven*, for example, is about the doorway [1973; Burden stood in the doorway of his Venice studio facing the boardwalk and pushed two live electric wires into his chest. The wires crossed and exploded, burning the artist.] And architecture would often kick off an idea about doing a performance in a specific part of the building. So, the piece at Ronald Feldman, when I was on the platform, came about because I found something very pure about that corner. [*White Light/White Heat*, 1975, in which, for 22 days, Burden lay flat on a triangular platform that was built in the southeast corner of the gallery, 10 feet above the floor and two feet below the ceiling. Nobody could see the artist, and vice versa.] The platform itself could be a piece of architecture. It could be a piece of minimal art. But it wasn't. It was just support for my body.

Wexner Castle, 1990, Addition of crenels and merlons to existing Peter Eisenman designed museum building, Installation at Wexner Center for the Visual Arts, Ohio State University, Columbus, Ohio. Commissioned for exhibition: "New Works for New Spaces: Into the Nineties," 10/6/1990 to 1/6/1991

— *In that case, did you actually become part of the structure?*
Absolutely. I did.

— *So, in the hierarchy we were discussing: where does performance fit in?*
Maybe it's three-dimensional. The performance pieces were essentially sculpture. I certainly don't see them as two-dimensional, although I know they're represented by photographs and a bit of text, now. In that sense, they're a little conceptual, because the photographs are not really satisfying, It's the written text that goes with the photograph that actually enables you to imagine the performance.

— *How do you feel about actually recreating a performance? I know that when Marina Abramović did* Seven Easy Pieces *at the Guggenheim, she wanted your permission to recreate* Trans-fixed, *and you said no.*
To me, something like that seems really silly. When you recreate somebody else's performance, it becomes theatre, and that has nothing to do with performance the way I conceived of it in the '70s. You can't do it over. I told her: 'If you're asking me, the answer is "no". But that doesn't mean you can't do it. You don't need my permission.'

— *Having said that, what kind of ownership do you feel you have over your performance work?*
Anybody can do anything over, but it won't have the same meaning anymore. I mean, I could do Joseph Beuys' piece with the hare [*How to Explain Pictures to a Dead Hare*, 1965] over again, but then it isn't a Joseph Beuys' performance anymore — even if it does have all the 'elements' of the original. So I'm not very interested in doing that. I think you become, maybe, an entertainer or something if you do. Laurie Anderson can do things over. I mean, she's a performer and an entertainer in some sense — a high-end entertainer. But I don't see myself in that way; that's not where my interest in art comes from.

— *A performance is ephemeral, in that sense. As well as a skyscraper like* What my Dad Gave Me, *because it's taken down after a certain amount of time. How do you 'hold on' to your work?*
You know, a lot of 'my energies' are spent writing letters. Making proposals, trying to negotiate, trying to describe things to the person on the other end. But that process makes me think about the work a lot. Putting it into writing is important, because it's a way to preserve the work, even if it's just an idea, a project that never happened. I think that's an integral part of art, really. I spend a lot of my time on it. I'm a desk artist.

www.gagosian.com

IT'S A BLADE STUCK INTO AN APPLE THAT SEEMS TO BE BLEEDING. OR NOT?

JUST MAD3 16-19 FEB 2012

Organized by:
artfairs

CONTEMPORARYARTFAIR

www.justmad.es

HOTEL SILKEN PUERTA AMÉRICA. MADRID. SPAIN.

MASTER LEVEL
bB

HIGH FIDELITY

BREAD & BUTTER BERLIN
tradeshow for selected brands
AIRPORT BERLIN-TEMPELHOF

PREPARE FOR A STRONG WINTER!

18–20 JANUARY 2012
www.breadandbutter.com

V

146

Chen Nong

THE MIRROR OF HISTORY

by Ana Ibarra

All images Courtesy of Galerie Alex Daniels
Reflex Amsterdam and Chen Nong

Chen Nong is a Chinese artist. Describing his work coarsely, one could say that he colours over black and white photographs. Outlined like this, it sounds like a simple enough process. The truth, however, is that each series will actually take him anything from seven months to two years before reaching conclusion. It is a hands-on process, in which the artist takes charge of every single stage. For this feature, we tried to find out just exactly what all this process implies.

Chen Nong, *Yellow River*, (one part of eight) preparatory sketch in watercolour and pencil on paper

His work is reminiscent of early black and white films coloured by hand. In fact, the whole process is not so different from making a film itself. There is a script, actors, the preparation of the props, finding the right location, the shooting and finally post-production. The photographs are like the frames of a storyboard.

The process starts with an idea. There is always an allusion to the past, a historic reference.

'We can never escape history,' the artist tells us, 'it is embedded in us, part of who we are and of what we become.' Connecting the past through the filter of his own imagination, he envisions the image he wants to recreate and starts sketching. It will take months of sketching before he manages to recapture the image that had previously come to his mind. But this is only the beginning, the point at which the whole process of recreating this image really begins.

As soon as he has finished sketching, he will start producing the costumes. These have all been decided beforehand – the sketch serving as a script to be followed to the letter. Finding props and costumes that will fit that script is then all about research and imaginative solutions, about improvising and finding ways of making these happen. He often goes to a wholesale market to find some 'finished or half-finished things', that he can then tweak, repair or paint to make them look like what he was first after. Sometimes, he designs the costumes and has them made by a tailor, as in the *Yellow River* series. At other times, he makes the costumes with rice paper and card board to obtain a special quality of paper, on which he paints with the same 'ink and wash' technique (and the same brushes) he will later use to colour the pictures themselves, as he did for the terracotta warriors of the *Three Gorges* series. The resulting costumes will look tactile, dramatic and real to the eye when the photograph is taken.

The site of the photograph has been studied carefully well in advance, taking into consideration the best season for the shooting and the feasibility of the site. When all the props are ready, everything is packed, everybody summoned, friends and models, all transported in big trucks to the location in a big expedition. He works with an old bellows camera he bought years ago in a second hand professional camera market. On site, the time for setting up the scene depends on the real situation of shooting location. With an old large format camera things go slowly: everything having to be perfect before he is ready to shoot. He will get his friends and models to pose, telling everyone the particular posture or gesture they are supposed to sustain, as well as where to look, how to act, etc., until he is ready to freeze that moment in time – one that matches the image he had previously sketched.

In the project of the *Dragon Bridge*, after he had rented a whole village in order to photograph peasants in their own typical setting, he rejected the whole photo shoot because the pictures didn't come out as he was expecting when developed, having to start it all over again with all the expense this implied. All these extra costs come from his own pocket. The artist will spend all the money he has earned in one project, on the next, living in humble conditions for his art. 'It is a natural choice,' Nong says. He is happy with his current life condition.

Back in the studio, he will choose the right picture, sometimes working on the negatives beforehand, taking out part of the images to leave enough room for applying colour at the final stage. Taking charge of every step allows him to control what he needs – even the printing is done by the artist in the dark room of his studio. In a process he describes as 'joy', he will see the image start to develop.

He will make three or four copies of each image, letting them dry before addressing the next and final step: the colouring. Using inks, like applying watercolours, he will add yellow, pink, blue, green, to the photographs, creating a kind of underwater image, a strange fluidity that runs through all his work. Adding colour can affect the photographic quality of the image, but it also creates a different dimension, a heavy colourful emotion, which engulfs the black and white and connects the photographs that will be displayed in a panoramic view, one next to the other.

Chen Nong tells stories through his photography, taking inspiration from a certain historical episodes, or from a dream-like scenarios. He explains his work as, ' I don't really want to freeze a moment, but to tell a story. But the interpretation of the work is up to the viewer.'

Chen Nong, *Three Gorges*, artwork consisting of 8 prints, silver gelatin prints, each uniquely painted each print 100 x 120 cm

Yellow River, (one part of eight) preparatory sketch in watercolour and pencil on paper

Yellow River shooting site

Chen Nong at studio for handmade prints

Yellow River shooting site

Yellow River shooting site

Chen Nong, *Yellow River*, art work consisting of 8 prints, silver gelatin prints, each uniquely painted each print 100 x 120 cm

Chen Nong, *Water Lilly*, silver gelatin print, uniquely painted, 100 x 120 cm

— *Can you tell us about your background?* My best art background memory is of a sunny morning when I was five years old, and I woke up to discover a little box that belonged to my cousin. I opened it and found small colourful watercolours, all laid tidily inside. I tried pushing several of the colours and they started to dance under the light. I was yielded by the parents and covered the box when the dance was over.

— *How did you first become interested in photography?* My family organized a spring excursion where we would be climbing a mountain when I was in junior grade five. My cousin wanted to take a photo in front of a strange stone we found on the trip, and I was fortunate enough to be carrying that miracle iron box, a camera. Naturally I clicked the button. I felt it was just the right moment. Such an operation fascinated me. However, after being developed, that photo turned out not to be that idealized moment when my cousin had closed her eyes and pointed and asked me to click.

I always enjoyed painting ceaselessly. I tried to study in the academy of fine arts for several years, took exams, but failed to get in. I then started working with sculpture and taking many photographs of artworks... And I started to fall in love with photography and taught myself how to take pictures by reading books about it. It seems to be easy for me when I have a deep interest. Photography is somehow a natural medium of expression for me.

— *What does photography bring to your work that other media cannot achieve?* Every media brings about a different experience. I finally found that photography allows me to show and express what I want in a way that is easy to control. It has since become my favourite medium.

— *Are there any artists that have inspired you?* Marcel Duchamp is the most admired and respected artist to me because he manages to bring art to a realm without boundaries, no matter which media he uses.

— *Is the history of China a source of inspiration for your work?* History always inspires your thought and action in its own profound way. History can never be replicated, or repeated, but my work serves as a reminder, or like a mirror.

— *How is your work process like?* Every work is started from action, with a brief image glimpsed in my imagination. After that, I sketch this image and keep on amending it, changing it, until I finalize it. Sometimes I will have to stop for a while, even in the middle of figuring out the sketch, but it all goes in a natural way.

— *Do you work with a large team or crew?* Yes, I do have a group of good friends, with whom I always drink and rarely talk about art. Still, I come up with many ideas and we have fun with them. Each team member has different skills and professions, but I summon them all up before the shooting, during the preparation of the costumes and props. The whole process for us is like a carnival. I am very grateful to my team.

— *Do you have a clear idea of want you want to achieve when you start a project, or does it develop with time?* It is like brewing wine. After I have finished the sketch, I start the shooting. During the process, the first plan develops as time goes by, taking into account the location, the timing, the people involved and the cost. Of course, it all runs under feasible conditions. It took me half a year to complete the sketch of *Yellow River*, and seven months to create and finalise for the props and costumes. It took about two years from start to finish.

The whole process for us is like a carnival

— *What are the different stages you go through before getting to the final artwork? Are these stages carefully planned and budgeted?* I don't particularly plan the different stages, or budget them... From past experience, it is only when making the final decision for the shooting, that I come up with a detailed plan and a rough budget, while having all always under control, and depending on feasibility.

— *How important is it that the costumes and the people look as if from a particular moment in the past?* I want the costumes and props I use in my works to transcend time and space, even if they are in a particular scenario. They are completed in a connecting series of one after another.

— *Do you visit the locations where your photographs are taken beforehand?* Yes, several times before I start sketching, and then after I have finished with it. The season and the location for shooting are the key to the planning and the staging. It is a time-consuming process.

— *Why have you chosen to work with traditional photographic techniques?* I just love it without choice. I always have the feeling that a new life seems to be born when the liquid flows with the black and white photograph appearing in the dark room.

Chen Nong *Climbing to Moon* opens Saturday 4th February 2012 from 5 - 7 pm. Show runs from February 4th - March 20th 2012
www.reflexamsterdam.com

züri
zür
ch

Text & Interviews
Corinne Olejak & Marc Valli

Photography
Dejan Savic

Zurich

There can be two views of Zurich. The first is that Zurich is not typical of Switzerland; the second that Switzerland is not typical of Zurich.

Zurich is the highly cosmopolitan, agitated centre of a highly stable, relatively calm and often provincial country.

OPENING TIMES

On our first afternoon, we sat at a terrace on the top floor of a building in the industrial quarter. Below us were at least eight parallel rail tracks, and not a minute would go by without a train rumbling past. We took the train on our way back a few days later. It left punctually at four past seven in the evening, and every carriage was filled with commuters, alighting in numbers at every city, even as far as Solothurn, about an hour away. The same would be taking place in every other train in every other direction, Luzern, Winterthur, St. Gallen, etc. Zurich is at the centre of a nervous system stretching over most of the Swiss territory. It is a city of movement, a deeply interconnected place. It is not just the creative heart of Switzerland, but also of a much wider international network. But this openness and interconnectedness will often put it at odds, as we shall see, with another aspect of the Swiss personality.

These statements, by the way, are not likely to endear me to readers in Basel, who are highly competitive with the Zürcher counterparts. In fact, when it comes to art, Zurich and Basel have been engaged in the aesthetic equivalent of an arms race. Twenty years ago, Basel was Switzerland's uncontested art capital. But things have changed since. Zurich is at the heart of the Swiss financial and banking system. UBS's HQ, for example, occupies almost a whole neighbourhood of eerie, shiny black and red buildings. Zurich's rise as a financial centre has run parallel with its rise as an art centre. Art became a popular commodity and the rise of the art market has also meant the rise of Zurich as an art capital.

Zurich today seems to have more galleries per capita than any other city in the globe and the quality of the work in these is generally high. That may not always play to the advantage of local artists though, as it is often the international art market, rather than the local scene, which is represented in those galleries. But this presents a challenge and an inspiration to local creatives and, if Zurich feels like such a vibrant and diverse centre today, that is definitely not just down to money, or the international art market.

Zurich's unique graphic design heritage and what became known as 'the Swiss Style' are there to prove it. After the war, influenced by Russian and European avant-gardes, Swiss graphic designers developed a unique graphic language: precise, efficient and, yes, very Swiss. A philosophy more than a style, it never went out of fashion and can still be seen in the work of countless graphic studios scattered around Zurich (and the world) today. There is still so much high quality graphic work being pro-duced in the city we would need a whole book to survey it. Note that, as I type these words, they appear on my screen in Helvetica – a typeface developed by a designer from Zurich (though, haha, the type foundry itself was in Basel...)

But let's come back to our starting point: openness and interconnectedness. Like every major city, Zurich is a city of immigration. But immigration is a hot political subject in this country. When asked about her impressions of Zurich, German artist Bettina Carl told us: 'the centre here leans a lot more to the right than in Germany. Sometimes it's upsetting when you see these black and white posters with the boots of immigrant people walking over the Swiss flag.'

She is referring to the now infamous as well as sadly effective black and white poster campaigns used by the Swiss far right party UDC. The party has campaigned on immigration with posters portraying, for example, white sheep kicking a black sheep out, black birds pecking at a Swiss map, or even a condom protecting Swiss people against foreign germs... The UDC would lose some ground in these elections, but it is still Switzerland's largest party in government. Carl, newly arrived in the country, could not help questioning the origins of this obsession, this resentment. Was it something innate in the Swiss? 'It is quite irrational. This is something I wasn't ready for. I thought that especially in somewhere like Zurich you wouldn't be that far away from mainstream political discourse...'

Zurich, however, the artists would nod, then suddenly say, 'Oh, but I don't know that one!'

And contrarily to what UDC politicians may believe, the Swiss too do migrate. They have always done so. My parents did, and so did my uncle (and later, so did I). More illustriously, Giacometti, Le Corbusier and Godard have all emigrated early on in their careers. Today, sadly, a steady migration of creatives into Zurich in the nineties and the early years of this century may be turning into an exodus. When we started this feature, seminal graphic artist Cornel Windlin was packing his boxes to move to Berlin. Andro Wekua had done the same. Ante Timmermans and his wife, Swiss painter Tatjana Gerhard, had moved to Brussels. But Zurich remains a very attractive destination. It is a city capable of inspiring surprisingly powerful physical responses, with its green hills, winding rivers, picturesque lake, varied architecture, and its spellbindingly quiet nights.

One evening, after having to walk half the city in order to find a place that would still serve food after ten, we found ourselves walking back to our hotel through an almost completely abandoned city. By then, it must have been around midnight. The silence was deep and unreal. One couldn't even tell if the river was still moving. Every now and then a solitary taxi or car slid by in the distance. In the ageless buildings by the side of the Limmat some windows were still lit (a solitary banker working late?), but there was just no one around in the streets. It was like being in a museum after closing time. Everything around us, from the walls and the décors to the floors and the

In Switzerland this 'outside' is a lot closer, and proportionally bigger, than in most places

Personally, I believe that this fear of the foreigner is not just innate, but almost unavoidable in such a small (and centrally positioned) country. It stems out of the need for its people to define themselves against what is 'not Swiss', what is outside. But in Switzerland this 'outside' is a lot closer, and proportionally bigger, than in most places. Switzerland lives in a state of permanent contradiction: while it depends on being connected to the rest of the world for its survival, it feels it is also constantly fighting not to be swallowed or engulfed by it.

Even Zurich, Switzerland's largest urban centre, is still a small place. When researching a guide like this one, you will inevitably be asked by the artists featured about who else is being included. And normally, once you start listing names, they will nod and, at one point, stop you to say, 'Oh, yes, I know that one.' In display cases, looked unquestionably tidy and neat, and beautiful, and untouchable, and often priceless. And that is the impression of Zurich I carried away with me: that of a modern museum. During the day anyone (foreigners included) is free to come in and wander around at leisure; every so often you are even allowed to change the displays or rewrite the labels. But the opening hours are strict. (MV)

Kreis 4

You won't find a lot of contemporary art in Zurich's city centre proper. You will have to cross the Sihl River into the Kreis 5 and Kreis 4 districts, and in particular the Langstrasse neighbourhood. This is a fascinating place, where a very large red light district also houses, alongside pick-up bars and terraces, most of Zurich's thriving art scene. The area itself could have been conceived by a Dada or Surrealist artist, a colourful mixture of sex and art, slick galleries sitting next to tropical cocktail bars with Brazilian hookers on their terraces, on streets named after dour religious reformers. It is also worth catching a tram and making a detour down west to check out the art complex of Albisriederstrasse 199A, which is temporarily housing the Migros Museum, Hauser & Wirth and the Bob Van Orsouw Gallery – these will soon be moving back to their previous address at Limmatstrasse 270.

1. Barbarian Art

Exemplifies Zurich's international/crossroads status with varied shows, often with Russian connections. Artists include: Trevor Guthrie, Andres Bosshard, Anne Lorenz, Daniel Gendre, Hannes Brunner, Jso Maeder, Marck Marck, Marion Strunk and Maurice Maggi. Trevor Guthrie's show closes on January 21st, followed by Vladimir Glynin's Re-constructivism photo series (end of January) Oksana Mas (February – March).

Bleicherweg 33
www.barbarian-art.com

2. Barbara Seiler

Barbara Seiler runs a tight yet multifaceted ship with passengers varying from the videos of Justin Bennett, the delicate paper works of Dina Danish, the paintings of Sander Van Deurzen and the hard-hitting monochromatic energy of artists such as Ante Timmermans (featured) and Marc Nagtzaam. Typically for Zurich, it is a highly international list. *Heimir Björgúlfsson* runs from January 14th to February 25th, and *Hamid el Kanbouhi* starts on the 3rd of March.

Anwandstrasse 67
www.barbaraseiler.ch

3. Bob Van Orsouw Gallery

A neighbour of the Migros Museum and Hauser & Wirth, the gallery has followed them to their current site, which is a bit out of the way and in an uninspiring location. But if the current location is not that exciting, the art makes up for it. The gallery functions like a box of surprises, with work varying from the unique drawings of Marcel Van Eeden to the thousands of self-portraits that make up Philip Akkerman's oeuvre, the multi-talented, multi-faceted Shirana Shahbazi, or the four-handed paintings and installations and other performances of duo Lutz & Guggisberg (featured). The gallery will be presenting two separate solo exhibitions: *Philip Akkerman: Lost & Ambulous*, and *Albrecht Schnider: Wieder Finden*, up to February the 4th.

Albisriederstrasse 199A
www.bobvanorsouw.ch

4. Galerie Brigitte Weiss

This small and friendly gallery is a reflection of Brigitte Weiss' passionate personality, always keen on uncovering new art artists, and never one, it seems, for compromises.

Müllerstrasse 67

5. Corner College

A lot has been happening in this space in the past two years: talks, book launches and intellectually challenging exhibitions with artists such as Karl Larsson, Philip Matesic, Julian Myars, Andrew Renton, Vanessa Joan Mueller.

Kochstrasse 1
www.corner-college.com

6. Fabian & Claude Walter Galerie

A rich and varied list of artists, from more mainstream works such as the aerial photographs of Georg Gerster (of Swissair posters fame), or the paintings of Alice Stepanek & Steven Maslin, or the sculptures of Dennis Oppenheim, to more challengingly contemporary works such as those of Sonja Braas and Andy Denzler.

G27, Grubenstrasse 27
www.fabian-claude-walter.com

Kreis 4

7. Freymond-Guth Fine Arts

Not necessarily so easy to find, this concrete structure, which breaks with the tradition of the gallery white cube, is one of the newer, most exciting players in the Zurich art scene. Artists include: Marc Bauer, Stefan Burger, Discoteca Flaming Star, Virginia Overton, Eloide Pong (featured), Tanja Roscic, Megan Francis Sullivan, Karin Suter.

Brauerstrasse 51
www.freymondguth.com

8. Haus Konstruktiv
(House for Constructive Art)

This large art gallery pays homage to the fact that the Constructive Art Movement had strong roots in Swiss soil through the work of multi-disciplinary exponents such as Max Bill, Verena Loewensberg, Camille Graeser and Richard Paul Lohse. The Foundation, housed in a former power station on the Sihl River, at-tempts to retrace the movement's influence by combining the works of artists belonging to the movement with those of contemporary artists and designers. The result is not always convincing though.

Selnaustrasse 25
www.hauskonstruktiv.ch

9. Hauser & Wirth

This gallery embodies the rise of the Zurich art scene, from local art gallery to international powerhouse, so much so that the actual Zurich gallery is now somewhat dwarfed by its various London and New York counterparts. A neighbour of the Migros Museum (and the Bob van Orsouw Gallery) it has moved with it to their current location on the slightly unexciting second floor of a corporate HQ, but it should be moving back next year.

Albisriederstrasse 199A
www.hauserwirth.com

10. Kunsthalle Zürich

Another major space living in temporary accomodation. Lead by highly influential artistic director Beatrix Ruf, the Kunsthalle has put together an incredible line-up, including shows on Rosemarie Trockel, Zobernig, Bruce Con-

ner, Walid Raad, and Kerstin Brätsch and Adele Röder. It reflects the vitality of the city in terms of showcasing new art and is very far from the compromises – those pleasing and entirely safe shows – put together by similar institutions in other cities.

Bärengasse 20-22
www.kunsthallezurich.ch

11. Migros Museum

Sponsored by Switzerland's ubiquitous discount supermarket, Migros (a Swiss institution, this supermarket chain also provides all kinds of night courses at affordable prices), this can be a bit of a disappointing experience at the moment. The gallery feels somehow restricted in its current location. Artists featured are definitely high-level, but one feels that the shows are sometimes slightly predictable and not always as exciting as they could be. The trip down to Albisriederstrasse is still made worthwhile by the combo of Hauser & Wirth, Bob van Orsouw and the Migros Museum. Good bookshop.

Albisriederstrasse 199A
www.migrosmuseum.ch

12. Rotwand

Working closely with its roster of artists, since its beginnings in 2007, Sabina Kohler and Bettina Meier-Bickel have been presenting consistently strong shows, ranging from the socio-political to the existential, or more free-flowing improvisations such as Thomas Müllenbach's show presenting the more than 600 watercolours he painted (always to scale) of the private view invitations he kept receiving (Halboriginal, May 2011). Their roster includes performance artist William Hunt, sculptor/installation artist Chiharu Shiota and some first class painters such as Klodin Erb, Sandra Gamarra, Tatjana Gerhard and the aforementioned Thomas Müllenbach (see profile in the next issue). Group show Big Fish runs from the 14th of January through to the 3rd of March, followed by Filib Schürmann.

Lutherstrasse 34
www.rotwandgallery.com

13. Schau Ort

A rare thing: a bright, beautiful and friendly gallery. Since its opening in 2009, Elisabeth Kaufmann and Christiane Büntgen have put together an exciting list of artists whose works combine the sensual and the conceptual, the present and the past. Perfect examples of this are the paintings of Yesim Akdeniz Graf, the collages and watercolours of Bettina Carl (featured), the paper works of Simone Schardt, the videos and installations of Seline Baumgartner, or the drawings of Irene Weingartner. The dog doesn't bite.

Müllerstrasse 57
www.schauort.com

14. Stephan Witschi

You may have to look for it in a slightly hidden alleyway, but it's worth it, as this welcoming gallery includes highly-accomplished painters such as Corinne Güdemann, Karoline Schreiber and Dieter Hall, or the haunting (and haunted) drawings of Thomas Ott. Robert Honegger's *Honegger's World – Paintings and Kinetic Objects* runs until February 10th, followed by *Andrea Bischof & Hermann Kremsmayer* from March 2nd – 28th.

Zwinglistrasse 12
www.stephanwitschi.ch

Bettina

Carl

At times, when studying in the German academic system – mainly focussed on political and conceptual art – Bettina Carl couldn't help wondering where her art fit. But the issues her work touches upon, from identity to the idea of nature, are nothing if not political.

Deities Of The Forest: L'être Suprême, 2010
watercolor, charcoal, pastel chalk on paper, 178 x 150 cm

Bettina Carl is originally from Bavaria. She first studied languages in Germany and Spain. She went to Berlin when the wall came down: 'it was a very special time...' It was in Berlin that she started to study art. 'I was always drawing, but I didn't go to art school until the mid nineties.' The foundation of a project space with two friends from art school was followed by a postgraduate course in critical studies in Malmö.

She moved to from Berlin to Zürich in 2007, for personal reasons. When asked about the differences between the two cities, she highlights the arresting juxtaposition between Berlin's uniquely troubled modern history, and Zurich's uniquely peaceful one. 'It's a peaceful and quite self-referential history. And this obviously has an impact on the mentality of the people. Zurich is more conservative. The centre here leans a lot more to the right than in Germany. Sometimes it's upsetting when you see these black and white posters with the boots of immigrant people trampling over the Swiss flag.'

She is referring to the poster campaigns for the very popular far right party UDC. Interestingly, ideas of origins and identities are never far from Carl's own work. Another parallel presence is the idea of nature, or rather, of 'nature as an idea, as the ultimate other for Western mankind – nature as a picture'. 'Nature as we experience it today is a landscape painting,' the artist tells us, adding that she cannot comment on a more real experience of nature, such as that of seeing, say, crops destroyed by storms. She is interested in all the artificial ideas we associate with nature. There is, for example, the mid nineteenth and early twentieth century German romantic notion of connecting the woods with a national identity. Or the idea of the 'femaleness of nature' – as exemplified in traditional landscape paintings featuring nymphs and languorous naked goddesses. 'An identity constructed by the bourgeois modern male subject, and yet another form of "otherness". But that is only a background to my work,' Carl hastens to add, a stage on which she gets her images to evolve, wandering, drifting between abstraction and figuration, between the present and the past, between irony and nostalgia.

The artist does this with particular lightness of touch. 'It is not coincidental,' she tells us, 'that I am not a painter in the traditional sense. When you are drawing the material aspects of the craft are not so present. Drawing is closer to thinking. It doesn't have this physical weight. It's closer to fiction. Paper meets my necessities very well. It has this ethereal, floating quality. Most of the work is done with various pieces of paper hanging simultaneously on the studio walls and echoing one another, so I suppose in that sense I also have a painterly relationship to the work.'

Deities Of The Forest: Moon, 2011
watercolor on paper, 40 x 30 cm

Paper meets my necessities very well. It has this ethereal, floating quality

'When I start, I have an idea of what I want a piece to feel or sound like. And then I go through a process of translating that.' She defines her work as a 'process of translating and becoming', while adding that 'there is an element of destruction in this "becoming", even in the very harmless way of covering what has been there before.'

I am strongly connected to traditions and discourses about tradition. And memory. Memory is so much more than what can be represented in verbal language.' But, of course, memories are always also part of our present, and her work describes, in vivid detail, these complex wanderings through the present and the past. 'It is an illusion to think that you can start from nowhere,' she ads. We are miles away from the UDC's black and white poster campaigns.

www.bettinacarl.de
www.schauort.com

Ante   Timmermans

Ante Timmermans gets about a lot, generally by car and often, it seems, with a sketchbook on his lap. When we first contacted his gallery, the artist was in Zurich. When we were in Zurich, he was in Berlin. We reached him (over the phone) in Gent, and finally, he sent us the images for this feature after a meeting with his gallery back in Zurich. We had come full circle, back to where he had begun at the Barbara Seiler gallery, deep in Kreis 4. Circles, in fact, play an important part in Ante Timmermans work.

Fict Fact, 2011, 180x120 cm

'The circle is quite important in my work – with its association to cycles and routines, etc. To give you an example: at a certain moment I was driving on the motorway in Brussels and noticed, at one of those busy crossroads, these very big lamps. They were something I would drive past every day, without noticing. So I made a drawing there and then, changing the lamp into a wheel. And then later I also noticed, while looking at paintings by Brueghel, that wheels were used to torture people. And that's how my mind works. It's always about making these connections and associations. There's always this movement in my work: starting, say, with a circle, then a circus, then playing. [Circuses in the artist's work, by the way, are not just playful, but also something one gets caught into; more Kafka than Degas.] But I also had a fascination for this clock, and the idea of control, bureaucracies, factories... I see my work more and more as playing with these systems.'

Systems are certainly something Switzerland has in abundance. The artist moved to Zurich for personal reasons: 'My wife is an artist with Swiss roots. In 2007, we decided to live in Zurich for a while, slightly outside the city. It was an interesting period...' He says, before adding, 'Interesting doesn't have to mean something "positive". There are a lot of rules, and systems, and structures.' Though he also points out that, 'Even now that I am living in Belgium, I seem to be working with people in Zurich more than with Belgian people.'

'I moved a lot in the last five years. First in Belgium, between various cities, then Berlin, Zurich. I had an opportunity to stay three months in New York. It's not some kind of strategy. I have just been following my work.'

Ante Timmermans is originally from Ninove, a small town between Gent and Brussels, 'a small town, an ugly town,' where he didn't have much contact with art or museums (except, he says, for Latin classes at secondary school). He then went to Brussels to study in order to become an art teacher, which is when he first realized the possibilities of the visual arts. This convinced him to continue studying and to go through art school in Brussels. After that, he worked for a few years as a teacher and worked for non-profit organizations. He was working full time while practicing as an artist. This is when one of the key themes, 'this every day routine that feels like a prison', emerged in the artist's work. 'I was working in the evenings and at weekends. Or I was making my drawings in trains, or in the car in traffic jams. I was trying to find my language as a visual artist. Then, in 2005, I applied to the Higher Institute in Antwerp for a postgraduate course. I gave up my normal job and had a studio for two years. I had made a decision to try to find my way as a visual artist. From there, I went to Berlin, and then to Zurich.'

527/2011
2011, 21 x 14 cm

**I try to draw in space.
I like the idea that someone
can walk into a drawing**

What are you doing? (Poesie der Langeweile), 2010,
spray and oil stick on paper, 180 x 120 cm

Architektur der Disziplin, installation view, 2010

Ante   Timmermans

489/2010, 2010, pencil on paper, 21 x 14.5 cm

Descendant

It's not like I have to draw every day, but I have to deal with how I think every day

He may deny that it is a strategy, but *movement* certainly feels like an important part of his modus operandi: 'I started to make my work when I was thinking in a car, or in a train. It's easy. All you need is a piece of paper and a pen. Then you start to make something visible. My work was always to do with a thinking process. Drawing is like writing. It's a very direct way of working. I never make sketches. My starting point is often an idea, or a working title, and the work grows from there.'

'I am not at all a workaholic. I cannot work if I don't have anything to say. It's not like I have to draw every day, but I have to deal with how I think every day. The studio is not just a working place, it is also a thinking place, a reading place.' He has once termed what he does, 'routine observations'. 'These are things you see every day and, at a certain moment, it stays in your head.'

While we are on the subject of travel and movement, we cannot help noting the fact that there are quite a lot of trains in the drawings. 'The train for me is more like this track, "le chemin de la vie" – otherwise I am a typical Belgian and prefer to travel by car... Maybe this stupid or romantic idea of travelling by car...'

If movement is a key element, so are games. The artist describes how he started to play with a Tangram game [note that a Tangram is an old Chinese dissection puzzle consisting of flat shapes, which are put together to form bigger, more specific shapes using several pieces], and a whole series of drawings, both abstract and figurative, were inspired by the game and the possibilities it offers. In the Tangram game we seem to have a good image of Ante Timmermans' art practice itself: a playful system, in which shapes and connections keep being formed, then lost, then reformed; differently, creating different meanings.

The Tangram pieces will often form mountains and factories – and in relation to these the artist mentions the Sisyphus myth as being often in the back of his mind. 'But I do not consciously look for symbols. They just come out of the process of working.'

The artist has been producing larger paper works, but these are often still just pinned to a wall. 'I like to keep that contact with the paper. My work evolved organically. I started making small drawings and when I was invited to participate in an exhibition, it felt natural just to pin these to the wall.' Though drawing on bigger formats, he tries to retain the proportions of a page. He says, 'At one point, I started making large format landscape drawings, and worked for long periods of time on one drawing, sometimes three or four months. And what I noticed since I started working with these kind of formats is that, because they have the same proportions as the smaller drawings, it is easier for me to think and work in a coherent manner.

It is a book format. And somehow, it is easier for me to think in those formats.'

His drawing practice does also involve sculptures and installations. These are generally made out of wire, emulating the language of line drawing. In fact, the artist refers to them as '3-dimensional drawings', and adds, 'I try to draw in space. I like the idea that someone can walk into a drawing. It is a form of investigation into what is a drawing. Or a form of zooming in and out.'

This drawing in space also includes directing shadows and using sound and movement, as in the piece, *Ludopticon*: 'It works in a short loop and connects to the idea of the wheel of fortune. My work seems to be moving more towards this installation kind of work. I love to visit exhibitions in which I am drawn completely into the mind of the artist. I like to combine drawings, 3D drawings and text works.'

Language is another significant presence in the artist's work. But, quite unusually, and in a way quite fittingly (as, again, it relates to movement and travel), he keeps switching between at least three different languages (French, English and German). 'At the beginning there were almost no words in my work. I was afraid to use them. I started to draw to visualize my thinking process. But I wanted to leave things open, avoiding big statements, whereas text is a lot more defined. I spoke French before, then I started speaking in English more and more often, then I learnt German. And I welcomed the opportunity to play in all these languages. This combination, these relations between words in different languages, makes it far more interesting to me. I like playing with words, connecting words, or even making new words. There are lots of texts and books around me at the studio.'

The words often remind one of graffiti on the streets of Paris in May 1968, which prompts us to ask the question of politics.

'I was expecting that question. There is a notion of protest in my work, that's true. But if I were a politician, I would be a very bad one. I doubt too much. I don't believe in one kind of truth. But maybe that's also political...'

We suggest that his work often embraces the language of protest and he admits that, 'Yes, but a subtle protest. A contradiction? No, I don't think so. I don't need to stand in front of people and scream.'

www.antetimmermans.de
www.barbaraseiler.ch

508/2011, 2011, ink and pencil on paper, 21 x 14.5 cm

Elodie

Pong

Elodie Pong was born in Boston, then came to Switzerland when she was seven years old. Later she lived a few years in Paris, and spent a couple of years in San Francisco. Her academic background is no less varied, having studied sociology, anthropology and theatre. She says that socio-cultural dynamics in art have always been of interest to her. She started being more seriously interested in art when, at eighteen, she met a group of artists from New York.

Untitled (Plan for Victory), 2006, video loop, 1min1 5s, courtesy of the artist & Freymond-Guth Fine Arts Ltd.

— *When did you come to Zurich?* I came here about seven years ago from the French speaking part of Switzerland, for personal reasons. I didn't intend to stay, but I'm still here.

— *Film, art? What came first?* Film, definitely. I grew up in America where film culture is a part of everyday life. Art was quite present as well, because as a child I was enrolled in a pilot school program that focused on creative expression.

— *Do you still remember your first camera?* It sounds so nostalgic! Even though it was only about ten years ago. It was a Digital8. And it was incredibly easy to play with. I thought it was great to just press 'REC' and then be able to see something over and over again on the tiny viewer.

— *How would you describe the relationship your work has with cinema?* The length of a couple of my films – *Secrets for Sale* [2003, 64 min.], and *CONTEMPORARY* [2011, 70 min.] – relate my work to a cinematic form; plus the fact that I prefer them to be watched in movie theatres. *Secrets for Sale* is a reflexion on what can be said, how it can be said, and to whom. It plays with the viewer's expectations, questioning the limits of what is acceptable. *CONTEMPORARY* is closer to the way I usually proceed in my installation videos: it makes reference to cinema and TV history – the emblematic qualities of stars, pop-icons, politicians and philosophers and the way they are part of our collective memory. Fusing personal and collective history, the film explores changing values and shifting identities in the wake of globalization in an era of copy-paste and postmodern appropriation culture.

  CONTEMPORARY is neither feature film nor documentary but bears the properties of both. My work refers to cinematic codes and language, but not necessarily in a historical manner. I suppose I am flirting with cinema while keeping my distance.

— *How would you characterize the difference between video art and film?* I think it's a question of narration, and perhaps a question of perception of time and space as well. It's a matter of expectations; the prospective experience of the viewers is probably different in the different settings.

  But boundaries are blurring – artists are making films and filmmakers are doing installations; it's a good moment to think about what the respective qualities are.

  Recently, I've been interested in the way a story can be told from various perspectives, expressing a range of opinions, all at once. I like a plot to have somewhat of a beginning and an end, but I think it's only logical that today,

Who said we're just empty suits?

I suppose I am flirting with cinema while keeping my distance

shoot now, ask questions later.

Even A Stopped Clock Is Right Twice A Day, 2008, HD video loop, 2min 36s, courtesy of the artist & Freymond-Guth Fine Arts Ltd.

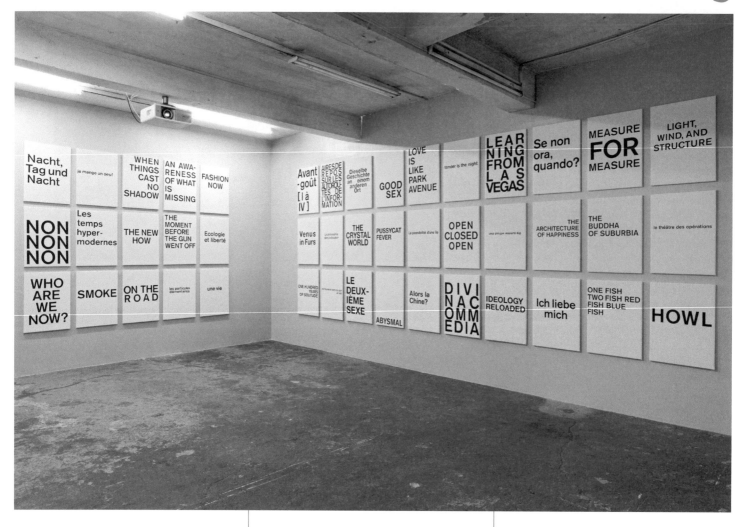

Coverology, 2011, installation view at Freymond-Guth Fine Arts Ltd.
and *Ersatz* videostill, HD video loop, 3min IIs,
courtesy of the artist & Freymond-Guth Fine Arts Ltd.

ideas should be perceived in bits and pieces, in a sort of individualized continuity. And that is definitely a challenge to linear narration.

— *Is your work carefully scripted?* I usually write scenes and dialogues, plus possible situations to try out. It depends on who I am working with, but I like to leave space for improvisation. I don't do storyboards, but the way the sequences are cut up and shot are discussed and roughly sketched with the cameraman.

— *How long do you spend filming, as opposed to editing?* I usually spend a lot more time editing than shooting. For me it's the most important step in the process. I enjoy working on things for longer periods of time so I can read as much as possible on the subject, meet people and learn more.

— *How do you find actors for your pieces?* I rarely do castings. Either I spot someone in a play, a dance piece, or a performance, or I work with people I've worked with before – in particular Carine Charaire, a French choreographer-artist.

— *You comment on your website that* The End *should be seen as something positive.* I was talking about a video, which is an anthology of film clips featuring the words 'The End'. It focuses on the endless negative space extending before and after the conclusion of each movie. Each scene's final image holds some residual trace of the film that ran before, carrying the imprint of its poetry, nostalgia, mystery or humour – provoking memories, or just a feeling of having missed something.

— Plan for Victory *is a particularly impressive feat, in aesthetic, conceptual terms.* The subtitle of this untitled video is the name George Bush gave to his military strategy for extricating American forces from Iraq in 2005. I sprayed the words — *Plan for Victory* — in fluorescent pink on a snow slope. They are then erased by an avalanche.

— *How did* Sincerely Yours *come about?* This video was made in 2006, following a residency in Alexandria. I had initially developed a project in which I wanted local people to ask me any questions they wished. The idea was to produce a reverse portrait of these people, through what they were interested in finding out about me. I couldn't realize my original idea, so I opted to use a fixed frame showing an empty wedding altar with changing lighting. The video image is interrupted now and again by sentences originating from the above-mentioned questions and deriving discussions. At the end, the image fades to black and the song *Be My Friend* by Majida El-Roumi can be heard.

— Death Valley – *I didn't personally see the show, but I got the feeling that you were trying to use irony in order to touch upon pretty heavy notions.* I'm not sure if the show was really ironical. But I do enjoy using humour when it fits a purpose. In this case, I just tried to set an apropos mood for the two installations. In the first room, on a wall which was blocking the entrance of the gallery, a video entitled *Even A Stopped Clock is Right Twice A Day* which was realized shortly before the economic crisis in 2008 presented itself. In this piece, a group of stuffed birds debate about globalization and the state of the world economy. The other room was painted red, and the windows were covered in red plastic film. Daniel Johnston's *Devil Town* song interpreted in a capella by a young woman could be heard.

— *Why use book titles as the raw material for your 2011 show* Coverology? The concept of *Coverology* concerns the relationship we have with our books – culture, knowledge and self-definition at a specific moment in time, but also as objects, fetishes or emotional landmarks. I used canvases for the text, and filled a room wall-to-wall with them.

The titles alone are a marker of all the latter. Randomly placed one next to the other, they create new worlds through associations and point out some traces of our trajectories, reverberating the entire spectrum of our – potential – thoughts and positions.

It was a lot of fun to play with the design options of the titles and yet let new meanings appear here or there, but the no-design – no graphic rules – rule for the whole collection of seventy two canvases actually made sense in epitomizing each book-slash-title and its specific significance.

— *'Fiction comes before reality' – does it?* Yes. Isn't everything a construction?

— *And finally, what's next?* I'll go to New York where I was just awarded a studio grant for a year. Other than that, I'm working on a project on perfume as the quintessential liquid modernity.

www.elodiepong.net
www.freymondguth.com

Sincerely Yours, 2006, video loop, 4min 02s, courtesy of the artist & Freymond-Guth Fine Arts Ltd.

Kreis 5 & Industrie Quartier

If in Kreis 4 art meets sex, in Kreis 5 art rubs shoulders with finance and industry. This can be done in a uniquely slick manner in galleries such as Eva Presenhüber and Peter Kilchmann (on the second and fourth floors, respectively, of the same building), or in a more improvised manner as is done at RaebervonStenglin, a gallery housed in a converted garage, next to a non-converted, still active one.

1. Eva Presenhüber

Located in the smart and modern Diagonal Building, right next to the Prime Tower, Switzerland's tallest building, Eva Presenhüber was, and still is, one of the lights leading the rise of the cosmopolitan Zurich art scene. Their list of artists is like a who's who of contemporary European art, from Swiss stars such as Urs Fischer, Sylvie Fleury and Beat Streuli, to ominous international names such as Angela Bulloch, Valentin Carron, Douglas Gordon, Candida Höfer & Co. Ugo Rondinone's monochromatic works (and particularly his intricate, large scale, black and white landscape paintings) made a particularly strong impression on us during our last visit. The gallery will be showing Oscar Tuazon from January 13th to February 18th, and Liam Gillick from March 2nd to April 7th.

Diagonal Building, Zahnradstr. 21, 2nd floor, www.presenhuber.com

2. Freitag Tower

In the early years of the century, Freitag became the must-wear brand for the trendy Zurich young, and now maybe not-so-young. True to the spirit of the Freitag brand, founders Daniel and Markus Freitag built their flagship in a tower made out of shipping containers, located by a flyover a few (intricate and highly urban) steps from the Diagonal Building, housing the Eva Presenhüber and Peter Kilchmann galleries.

Geroldstrasse 17
www.freitag.ch

3. Galerie Francesca Pia

Plenty of visually sumptuous and conceptually challenging shows have come out of this slick gallery, which is still able, some twenty-odd years later, of producing surprises. Another mandatory stop in the art visitor's list. Its very strong artist list includes: Aloïs Godinat, Wade Guyton, Fabrice Gygi, Jutta Koether, Kaspar Müller, Bruno Serralongue, Joseph Strau.

Limmatstrasse 275
www.francescapia.com

4. Galerie Lange+Pult

Another gallery along Limmatstrasse, Lange+Pult will often feature impressive, high-level shows. Oscilating between 2D and 3D, and usually rather slick, the art varies from Lilian Bourgeat's witty experiments with scale to Mathieu Mercier's soft minimalism and Pietro Mattioli's complex compositions.

Limmatstrstrasse 291
www.langepult.com

Kreis 5 & Industrie Quartier

5. Mark Müller

The gallery – which has moved into a light and spacious new building between Limmatstrasse, the Limmat and the Museum für Gestaltung – has been, for over twenty years now, one of the most consistently distinctive galleries in Zurich. The gallery has fostered original and varied careers such as those of Sabina Baumann (see interview) and Reto Boller, or those of a strong group of abstract painters including Urs Frei, Katharina Grosse, Joseph Marioni, Judy Millar and François Morellet. Markus Weggenmann's *Paintings* runs from January 14th to March 3rd, Joachim Bandau's *Alles nur Illusion* opens on March 10th.

> Hafnerstrasse 44
> www.markmueller.ch

6. Museum für Gestaltung (Design) Zürich

Visitors to the main building will possibly be disappointed in not finding many traces of Switzerland's rich graphic heritage. (For that, you would have to cross over the road to the Plakatraum on Limmatstr 55.) You will, however, usually find interesting alternative exhibitions, which would not necessarily find their place in a contemporary art museum, from the work of illustrators and designers to that of architects and urban planners. It is also a good place to buy Swiss graphic design posters at twenty-five francs (a bargain is pretty hard to come by in Zurich). *Black and White – Designing Opposites*, an exhibition looking at the role of black & white in art, fashion, design and architecture, from Modernism to today, runs until April 3rd.

> Ausstellungsstrasse 60
> www.museum-gestaltung.ch

7. Galerie Nicola von Senger AG

This impressive gallery on Limmatstrasse can host original shows by talents such as Roger Ballen, Beni Bischof, Pascale Birchler, Madeleine Berkhemer, Thomas Feuerstein and Hannes Schmidt. Definitely worth a stop.

> Limmatstrasse 275
> www.nicolavonsenger.com

8. Peter Kilchmann

On our visit we were treated to a very moving show by rising Swiss art star Zilla Leutenegger, in which she had managed the feat of disconnecting us from our environment (the Diagonal Building is as far from the intimate landscapes evoked in the artist's work as anything could be) and welcoming us for a few moments into distant corners of her memory, which was a surprisingly rewarding experience. The gallery also shows the work of Andro Wekua, the Georgian artist, who used to be based in Zurich, but has now, along with many other artists, drifted towards Berlin. Other names in the roster include: Rita Ackermann, Jochen Kuhn, Valerie Favre, Andrian Paci and Tercerunquinto. Javier Téllez shows from January 19th to February 25th, followed by shows with Bernd Ribbeck and Bruno Jakob, both opening on March 8th.

> Diagonal Building, Zahnradstr. 21, 4th floor
> www.peterkilchmann.com

9. RaebervonStenglin

This exciting new gallery is housed in a converted garage, right next to real, functioning one. No signage indicates its presence, or differentiates it from the neighbouring workshops, and you will have to lean against the windows to find it. The location may seem marginal, but the art isn't. From the restless talent of Saâdane Afif, and the refinement of Susanne Kriemann, to the more meditative works of Sofia Hulten and Ivan Seal, all of it is of excellent quality. If you can find your way, and then find someone in... (opening hours are, theoretically at least: 12-6 Monday to Friday and 11-5 on Saturdays) make sure you stop by.

Pfingstweistrasse 23
www.raebervonstenglin.com

Norm

I have met Dimitri Bruni and Manuel Krebs of Norm over a decade ago, and I remember thinking, 'Wow, these young guys are serious!' I have rarely met two more determined visual artists. They knew what they wanted to do, and had clear views as how to go about it. They were 'ambitious', but not in the sense that this was so often understood in those heady days at the height of Brit Art. It was not fame they were after. What they had were artistic ambitions and an aesthetic agenda. It is therefore refreshing to find them again, twelve years later, and discover that the ambition and the determination to do significant work on their own terms is still very much there.

Superficial, 2010, poster/exhibition project for Festival d'affiche Chaumont and Triennale de Milano, 64 posters

— *The two of you met at art school. How was that?* We met in 1991 on our first day at art school. Our class was small: we were only eight students, everybody was close. During school we started publishing a magazine, which somehow lead us to open our own studio once we finished school. The time at art school was very important – before that we didn't really have an idea what graphic design was. We spent a lot of time looking at things, talking about what was good and what was bad. We have the impression that, back then, fewer visuals were available. Books were the main source. We were in the library of the school and saw everything for the first time. We remember looking at the work of Max Bill, Donald Judd, Kurt Schwitters and Tadanori Yokoo, soaking in references.

— *Is Zurich a good place to be graphic designer?* We moved from Biel to Zurich to open our studio. There were several reasons. One was certainly that there was work in Zurich – more than in Biel, that in Zurich people are relatively open-minded in terms of graphic design, that clients are aware of the necessity of the designer and that there is a quite vivid exchange between other designers, artists, etc.

We are in Zurich-West. In this neighbourhood, you used to have the industry. When we came here, ten years ago, the rents were quite low and many of our friends were around. We came from a small town and this part of Zurich felt very urban. There were many improvised and independent places. But this has changed a bit, it's always the same story: many buildings have been renovated or were removed for bigger office towers. We still like it here, things are changing – that's ok, they have to.

— *How do you two work together?* We talk a lot, hardly ever long conversations, but many small bits through the day. When we started the office we decided to have our working tables side by side and have kept it like that since. This has influenced the way we work: we often look at the same screen, deciding whether this or that works better. Graphic design is all about taking decisions from morning till evening. Replica? Full-Bleed? Black? Bigger? Working with somebody you fully trust saves a lot of time. Whenever we both agree on a decision, we don't need to question it any further. On the other hand, we are more and more interested in things on which we do not agree. Towards one another we are both reviewers and allies.

— *Your work is very coherent, stylistically speaking. How do you achieve that?* At a certain point we realized that we were not interested in switching visual languages. We realized that 'anything goes' in terms of references is wrong, because it leads to a 'mediocracy'. We prefer exploring an approach in depth.

We like clear choices: in the Pantone formula guide wheel, we only use the first four pages, where red is red and blue is blue

Norm

— *Who are your main clients?* Over the last two years, we have revised the entire corporate identity of Swatch – from logo to corporate typeface over stores and ads, to umbrellas and tiny pieces on watches. We are currently finishing the design manual that will cover everything you can think of. Another project we also started almost two years ago – and that will last until December 2012 – is the signage for the new Louvre in Lens, a small town in the north of France, built by Sanaa Architects. We reached our limits with that project, caught between the excessiveness of French bureaucracy, Japanese minimalism and the megalomania of the Louvre.

— *What do you look for in a client?* We like to be the client ourselves: this always works very well. There are also relations with the artists we have worked with, among others Peter Fischli and David Weiss, Simon Starling and Christian Marclay. What makes a relationship work is a two-way exchange, both parties being open to be influenced and inspired by one another.

— *Now, as ten years ago, black & white seems to play an important part in your work.* We like the idea of structure over surface. It matters for us to take clear decisions: we don't like things to be in-between. We like black & white for the biggest possible contrast; a design should always work in black & white. Colour is possible, but there also... we like clear choices: in the Pantone formula guide wheel, we only use the first four pages, where red is red and blue is blue.

— *Do you give yourself stylistic rules?* Rules are very important, not only stylistic ones – we have rules for everything, from A to Z. We like to have rules; we think it's easier to evolve within certain boundaries, and we think it's important to be aware of the rules you are applying – there are certain things we almost do automatically and others we would never do.

— *Do you always think about what you do, or do you sometimes act rather intuitively?* We always talk – meaning 'think' – about a project before we do anything. We try to define and regulate as much as possible before we even touch the mouse. We search to have clear criteria to judge a project. We avoid making decisions based on beauty, we try to make decisions based on whether the project corresponds to the initial set of rules, or not.

— *While researching this feature, I realized that a large number of Swiss artists and designers didn't have websites, or had just holding pages, such as yours. Why is that, do you think? Is it because they don't need foreign clients, or features in foreign magazines? Or is it wanting to deal with people in their own terms?* That's right, we are not so interested in having an online portfolio that reduces our work to a number of pictures. We always thought of our website as a complementary element to the print work we do, but then the version we had done a long time ago, something like 2002, had been online ever since, and we just couldn't find the time to revise the project. We often talk about things we'd like to do on our website, but it's just that we don't have the time to develop it. The version we have now – with nothing – just seemed to be a better choice than something we are not sure of. We will be working on it, very soon.

www.norm.to

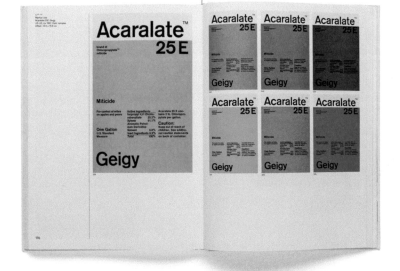

Corporate Diversity, 2010, book
Museum für Gestaltung Zurich, Lars Müller Publishers

Bruce Lee, 2005, poster

Sabina Baumann

Sabina Baumann's studio is in a clean, well-maintained building on the industrial outskirts of Zurich. We climb to the fourth floor, and then one more, to sit on the terrace of an elegant canteen (also run as a social project aiming to help women out of long term unemployment). It is a clear afternoon and, from the terrace, one can see the whole of Zurich: the green hills across the tracks, the industrial quarter, and even some of the old city centre. As we speak, an endless procession of trains runs to and fro on the tracks below.

Endlos, from the series: Portrait, Landschaft, Körper, 2009, pencil on paper, 42 x 42 cm

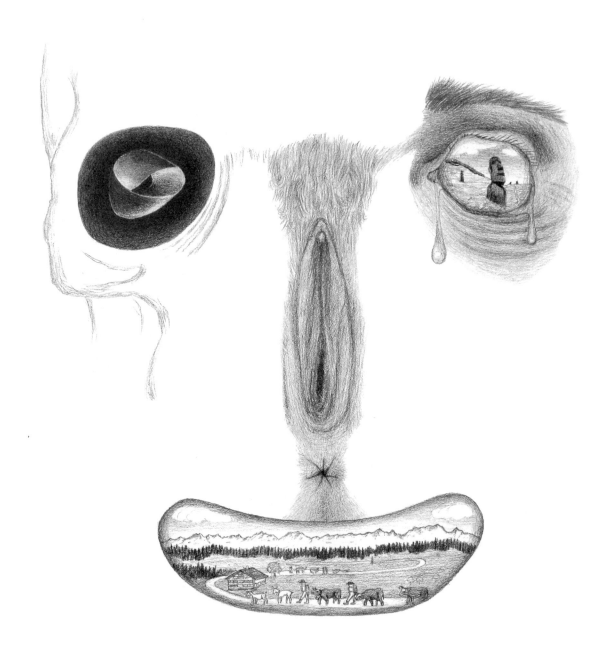

'I have been in this building for ten years.' Sabina Baumann tells us, over the sound of the trains. 'There are all kinds of artists in the building, from film technicians to all kinds of crafts. If you need anything, it's in the house. If you need cheap workers, say, carpenters, anything, you can find them in-house.'

It is a housing cooperative and the studios are co-owned by their tenants. This is an enviable situation in a city like Zurich. 'I never have to move out again. I have moved so many times... I am happy I can stay here.'

The artist appears to have found a good balance in her practice: 'I need to do the same things, always, because I think everything else is unsteady, unstable. I need a routine, otherwise I get lost.'

Baumann is originally from Wettingen (not far from Zurich) and has lived in the capital for about twenty-five years. 'The art scene, the queer scene, everything that is important to me is here.' But things have changed a lot in Zurich during that period. 'In those days, the art scene was very small. Basel was much bigger. And then came Hauser & Wirth, off spaces, and later the Migros Museum and many more galleries, and the art scene suddenly grew.' I mention Berlin, and the fact that many artists seem to be moving away from Zurich to the German capital, and she replies that, 'There was a migration to Zurich before that. Artists came to Zurich as it grew. Berlin is possibly better for an artist, cheaper, and more political, whereas here it is rather commercial.'

When asked if she finds any typically Swiss traits in her own work, she hesitates, 'If I look at the work of Swiss artists such as Pipilotti Rist and Fischli/Weiss, which I used to like when I was younger – they have a sort of a playful kindness and an irony, which I think is quite Swiss.'

This 'irony', which can sometimes turn political, does also extend to her sculptural work and moves around the juxtaposition of disparate elements, on an almost a surrealist model. A good example of this can be found in an installation in her current show. While doing research around the peace sign, she found out that it had become widely known through the post-war campaigns for nuclear disarmament. So her next show will feature an urn, which will have its ashes scattered on a green background of acrylic colour mixed with glitter to form a peace sign.

Interestingly, she seems to have resolved the conflict between art and politics in her work by dividing it in two: the more aesthetic/poetic works (i.e. her drawings), and works of about gender and queer politics, which are done in a more direct manner.

Baumann teaches, 'about twenty per cent of my time. Teaching made me more comfortable socially. It forces me to interact with people. I learn a lot from those I teach. I get a lot of information back.'

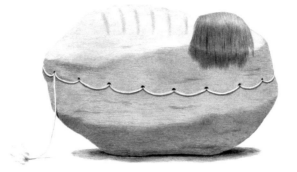

Untitled, 2008, pencil on paper, 88 x 130 cm

Drawing is somehow the most subjective thing you can do

Leben, from the series: Portrait, Landschaft, Körper, 2009, pencil on paper, 42 x 42 cm

Sabina   Baumann

Baumann is something of a late bloomer. She was already twenty-five when she went to art school, thirty when she came out. 'I don't have a very straight biography,' she adds. Baumann used to work in a completely non-artistic environment beforehand. 'I never thought I would become an artist. I had a boring job and didn't know what to do. I was drawing a lot of comics. I used to draw the people I worked with. Then someone suggested I go to art school.'

Coming to art school from a non-cultural background, she 'had the feeling that there were all these different worlds just next to each other, that didn't fit together, didn't understand one another.' The same thing was clearly reflected on a worldwide scale. 'The tv itself was like a sampling machine.'

She was always struck about the fact that, 'You are born somewhere, and that's an accident. And so much of your identity is determined by that. This was before the discourse on identity became so prevalent. But for me that was always a central issue, and all I do relates to that. From very early on at art school, I tried to find a language to explore that. I do it by using different style fragments and quotations, which I then draw. When I was younger my main inspirations were what you find in magazines and comics... and Minimal Art. For me, Minimal Art was interesting, but very one-sided – five years of Minimal Art at art school...' she says, shaking her head.

'At the time, the information flow was becoming bigger and bigger. I was cutting images from newspapers and magazines, and then it became Google, Google, Google... [laughs] I making little sketches and collages. But that kind of research is only the surface. These collages are like stories moving in every direction.

'Drawing changes the material. It would be very different if I used photographic material directly into a collage. Drawing is somehow the most subjective thing you can do. It always has this personal touch.' There seems to be an almost a therapeutic side to how she talks about her drawing practise, 'It goes through me. I try to deal with it in a way that is good for me. And maybe if it is good for me, it is also good for others.'

You may be seeing, as I first did, the drawing on a page (or a screen), but the originals are on a bigger scale, and that changes one's perception drastically. Not only do they have much greater impact, they also come alive in a different way.

I blurt out the words, 'It's like a bigger than life comic-strip.'

Baumann corrects me, 'More like: as big as life'.

And she's right. The elements grow into almost living, flesh and blood creatures. She says she works through 'loose connections,' but the clashes are not just the usual conceptual clashes of a collage. Disparate objects suddenly find themselves bathed in the same element: a Henry Moore sculpture rests by a Philip Guston figure surrounded by signs and symbols, scientific apparatuses, celebrities and real people. The mood varies and the works lend themselves to a multitude of meanings. These composite drawings will then be hung in clusters, creating yet further meanings and associations.

'It is like an endless story. And you will never understand the whole.'

The show 'Finger aus Licht' by Sabina Baumann is at the Mark Muller Gallery between the 19th of November 2011 to the 7th of January 2012.

Hafnerstrasse 44
8005 Zurich
+41 (0) 44 211 81 55

www.sabinabaumann.ch
www.markmueller.ch

Little Boy Hop, Steineserie, 2009, pencil on paper, 132 x 150 cm

Untitled, 2008, pencil on paper, 152 × 120.5 cm

Andres Lutz & Anders Guggisberg

Partnerships in art are uncanny, intriguing affairs, a game of hide and seek with authorship and identity, a play of light and shadow between personalities. This can certainly be said of the partnership of Andres Lutz and Anders Guggisberg, whose fate it seems to be to play that game even with their first names (a dyslexic writer's worst nightmare). Their work skips freely between dimensions (from 2D to 3D) and materials, between modes (from highly intense and image-laden films to casual stand-up performances), between the conceptual to the sensual, jumping from the humorous to the heart-breaking (sometimes within a single photographic frame).

Die Zeitmaschine/The Time Machine, 2011, oil on canvas, 160 x 200 cm, courtesy Bob van Orsouw Gallery

We are glad to say that we now think we have safely established that it was Andres [Lutz] who picked us up at the Dietikon's station and Anders [Guggisberg] who walked back with us after the interview. Dietikon is an industrial suburb, and delivery trucks are parked in front of what used to be the last independent local brewery (sadly now owned by a major international brand). The studio is spacious – you could easily fit a bowling alley with at least three tracks inside it. Like different classes at a school event, all kinds of objects, from wooden sculptures to papier-mâché décors, have been allotted different areas of the room, and are greedily competing for our attention. Note that, after spending a good part of our visit trying to work out exactly who was Andres and who was Anders, and then trying to establish which replies belonged to whom, we finally decided to give this up and mostly let the interplay of their personalities do the job; as they do, to such rich and lively effect, in their own work.

'Where to start' is a question we also asked ourselves when faced with the diversity of the duo's output. So we started – Lutz and Guggisberg don't seem so bothered with hierarchies – by leafing through one of their photography monographs.

'Impression from the Interior,' Lutz tells us, 'is a series of black and white photographs, a bit pseudo-ethnographic, about the mountains and countryside all over. Everyone can shoot pictures, I think, but the work then is to edit them, choose, find the right number, make the sequences and give them titles. It's a bit like journalism, or collecting. Photo work has lots of space and everybody has his own.'

'Some photos are taken because they fit well with the subject or the title. But it can also be just because we liked what we saw. Then we collect them and make them fit together. As, for example, this one: *Fish at the Lake*, which is not Fish *in* the Lake... and *Christmas Wolf* – that was taken from a pharmacy's window at Christmas time.'

We are now walking by the main wall, on which large-scale paintings are hung, with more experimental 2D works on paper and canvas, laid out on the floor.

'We have a collector coming tomorrow and we hope to get rid of some paintings!' Andres Lutz explains, before disappearing at the back of the studio, calling out, 'Anders! We got a visit!'

They started to do painting in 2005 by taking photographs from newspapers. Before that, they were doing mainly sculpture or installations.

'You come to this point of collaboration when you get used to the other and are able to let things develop, to let things happen and go. When you paint something, you have to be ready to discover that what you did changed, as the other will come and cover it with new elements.'

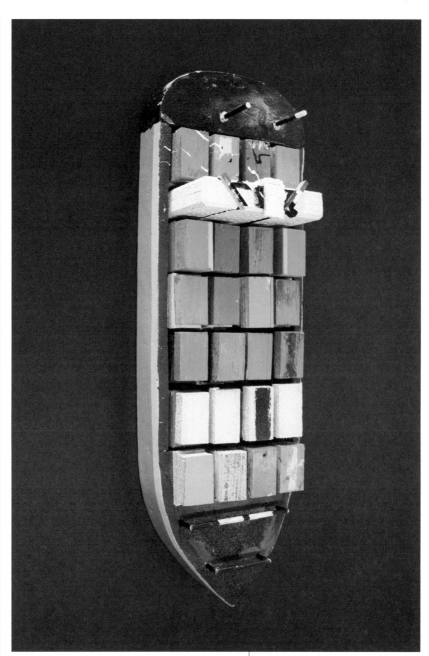

Maske/Mask, 2010, wood, paint, styrofoam, 67 x 22 x 15 cm, courtesy Bob van Orsouw Gallery

Doing art with a programme these days can be a bit ridiculous, as everything is copied-pasted, copied-pasted anyway

Andres Lutz & Anders Guggisberg

'And painting is very much more like the idea of the artist as the hero, isn't it?'

'Yeah, individual, is he a genius, or not a genius!'

'Do you have a plan, sketches?'

'No, no...'

'You're kidding!'

'No, it's actually done without any [planning]. The subjects are always more or less figurative: for example, artists – the old northern paintings we adore, like Brueghel and Bosh, footage from newspapers, photographs that we copy on canvas and then continue somewhere else. Doing art with a programme these days can be a bit ridiculous, as everything is copied-pasted, copied-pasted anyway and every-where, and subsequently it's hard to find something new.'

The painting we are looking at began with a theme inspired from Brueghel's Hunters in the Snow, but a very contemporary and impatient hand (Lutz's? Guggisberg's?) has added smoke, alongside other disturbing contemporary shapes, until it veered towards something more akin to the Cohen Brothers' Fargo...

'It's much easier,' Lutz explains, 'to manage photo work as two people, or in a group as architects or advertisers do, than with painting, which has a specific ground where one single artist is in individual expression. Painting is a challenge for us.'

Meanwhile, behind us lurks a crowd of wood and papier-mâché sculptures, with shapes reminiscent of animals, artificial technologies (detectors and the like), eggs, which were originally part of a stage set.

'Last Saturday we had a comedy show in Winterthur. It's folk humour in Swiss German dialect, though we couldn't really go in the countryside with that, or on a TV show – that would be too weird.'

'In Zurich it's always a bit difficult to use this word but it has some Dada elements. This tradition will be part of the comedy, not as a concept, but more for the experimental potential that Dadaism gives.'

'In the past few years, we've been doing lots of paintings, installations and sculptures. So performing little things like we do, feels like having some fresh air.'

Comedy is in fact Lutz's background, while Guggisberg's is sound and music – the artist composed the soundtracks to a lot of fellow Zurich artist Pipilotti Rist's pieces, including her recent feature film Pepperminta, *2009. The two met in Zurich in 1996.*

'He was doing a lot with Pipilotti [Rist], while I was doing my comedy work. Our other work wasn't the central thing, yet. With the years, it became our main thing. Later on, Anders [Guggisberg] helped me find a new studio and did a second, then a third show with me. This is how we kind of started working together, but without any contract or fixed plan. We're not a couple in life either, just two guys working together. We started slowly, in an easy-going and relaxed way. And, you know, in Switzerland, you have a relatively good situation as an artist, with different levels of support – city, canton, federal.'

'We don't travel much. We feel good to live and work in a place. It's probably also easier in terms of working in collaboration. We have time to think, discuss what we do and time to settle things and finish them. It's not that we're against travelling, because we like to do it as well, but we like to be more settled.'

'Everyone is running everywhere all the time; they go here and there and move to Berlin, then come back for two months and then move again. Some others go to India. Of course, it's quite interesting. I've been to Beijing or Buenos Aires myself, but on the other hand, somehow, what's the benefit at the end of the day?'

'It has also something to do with private things, priorities. I've a family here and I feel myself more materialist. Being away from my things would be a problem. I would need so many things with me... I'm not a nomad, definitely not.'

'The concept of nomadism is something very beautiful: the idea of aborigines having just a little kangaroo stomach with everything in there and all his possessions known by heart... But not the airplane thing...'

'Being two of you – does it help you in terms of motivation and rhythm?'

'We've been working together for years and it's not always, "Oh..." It's more like a marriage with all the advantages, and sometimes you get on each other's nerves, in a very, very normal way. As I said, we were not in love, or a couple, it just happened. Nowadays, it's not that special anymore to work in collaborative forms. Look at a Fischli and Weiss, for example.'

'The focus is on the result. In the production of movies, for instance, the identification is with the product. This is a very interesting part of this work: you identify something that is not only you; it's not self-centred.'

'Do you sometimes feel a bit frustrated that you'd like to do something, say, for instance, more confessional? Do you sometimes work separately?'

'In our collaboration there's space for that. In our catalogues, there's lots of work that was done separately. But we won't tell you what, because this is not what we're after. It's not important for you to know the percentage of each individual in the work.'

'I like to compare this collaboration with a design studio, two graphic designers, actually. When you're alone as a graphic designer, it's hard: you can't get sick, etc. We need each other: when one can't work, the other can help and, well, it's a studio collaboration, a little company and a label.'

'Do you have arguments?'

'I was mentioning the word "marriage"... I don't need to say anything else! Of course, it happens in a very normal way.'

'You mentioned the words "easy going"...'

'"Easy going" in the sense of entertaining ourselves a bit, though it's also a struggle and working can be tough too. The art world and its market are hard, and not so good at the present time.

Weihnachtswolf/Christmas Wolf, 2011, photograph, courtesy Bob van Orsouw Gallery

> It's more like a marriage with all the advantages, and sometimes you get on each other's nerves, in a very, very normal way

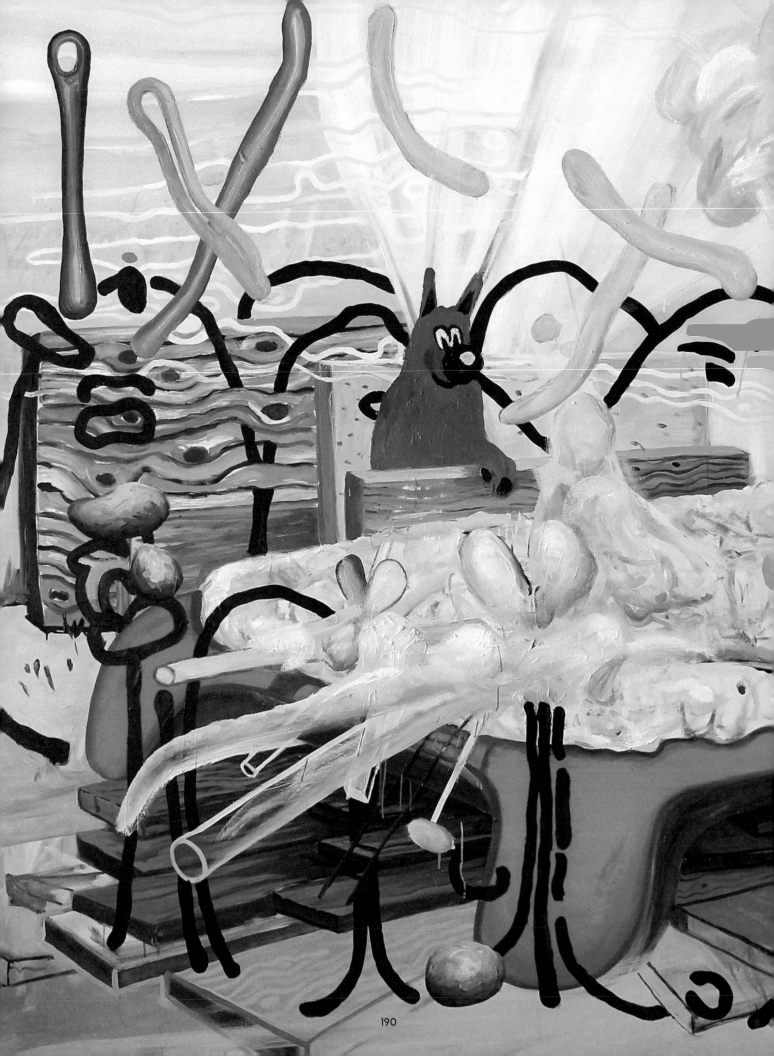

Der Schöpfungstag/Day of Creation, 2011, oil on canvas, 190 x 240 cm, courtesy Bob van Orsouw Gallery

Andres Lutz & Anders Guggisberg

Being an artist is really serious... It's super capitalist, and you've got to produce. And yes, we also have a big expensive space – this studio – and need to sell in order to keep working in it. As an artist, you're very much part of a meritocracy, not only on the working side, but also on the selling side. So it's not always easy going.'

'But then, besides the pressure everyone has on his shoulders, there's the work itself, and there, there's a lot of satisfaction.'

'And there's irreverence and humour in your work.'

'But humour is something difficult to talk about; it's like freedom. Somehow, the more you talk about it, the more it disappears.'

'When you have fun doing something – that's something. It's already a good indication that something is happening. But it's not a concept. You're not wrong: we try to make people have fun with our work. We don't have anything against people being entertained.'

'Your work seems to be layered and it feels that often the first layer is humour. For instance, you showed me the picture Fish at the Lake *and it feels it makes you smile first, then when you realize what it means, you feel sad.'*

'It's not only funny, but also sad, or a bit tragic.'

'And they're "at" the lake...'

'A funny name for a sad situation.'

'It's like the wooden bird sculptures we made. First, it was a scene, then we made a video for a show, and for that we thought we had to burn something. Something had to happen. It was not a concept. We did burn one of those birds and we liked very much the result. And this brought us to think it would be nice to have them all burnt. The circumstances made it happen.When we got a show, where we had a bigger place, we burnt the wooden birds one by one, and after a week, we had more than a hundred burnt and mutated birds. They looked as funny as comic characters, but at the same time, these weird charcoal fellows looked so tragic... I think this gives a good idea of the development of our work, step by step, but also about how it can be here or there, in terms of the projection of possibilities, in our lives. Actually, people asked us if it was a representation of our life, or if this was an art scene. It was a funny work to do and, sometimes... we were lucky with the result. It's very simple and strong, and has nothing to do with Switzerland anymore. Everybody understands it, or has a possibility of understanding it in its own way; there's no barriers anymore.

The artists embarked upon this work during the bird flu epidemic, but also while the Iraq war was raging, and it bears an obvious connection to the images of the bodies of disregarded Iraqi soldiers – victims of areal bombardment.

As in any partnership, the jokes are often private jokes. Only in their case, this can be pushed very far. *For example, the two have been working, for some ten years now, on a private library of some 300 or 400 books. The artists invent the authors, the publishers, the titles, the series they belong to, the design style.*

'We also integrate paintings or sculptures in them, like an image catalogue. We made them with the idea of the cheap novels you can buy in kiosks.'

After reviewing the books, we can't help wondering at the artists' productivity, and can't help asking if they are not sometimes tempted to just have a drink and do nothing?

'I'm not so good at that. On the other hand, when the weather is nice, I sometimes have a problem with working. As I said, I like to go walking.' *On our way from the station Andres Lutz told us how he liked walking in the mountains.* 'But the perfect situation is to work and not realize it is work, and be amazed about what's happening. That said, we do sit around and talk, a lot.'

'How about Zurich, is it a good place to be an artist?'

'We are the generation that was lucky. For sure there was this big boom in London, New York, and Zurich was the very central place in Switzerland. It was a good time for us. The euphoria of our generation is a bit over now, and we became again quite normal. It was in the end of the eighties. I came out of my punk lifestyle, had studied art and was not particularly ambitious. The plan to go in a gallery was not really there, it was more of a coincidence.'

'Switzerland was really late in terms of the development of art schools, because there's a big tradition of sending the students to Paris or Munich and it has no academy. The art school history is still very young here and every year, there are many new artists coming from abroad to study here in Zurich, or in Germany. It has become hard. Because of the boom there's more ambition and optimism – and disappointment as well, as the market has become harder and a bit smaller. Plus schools put pressure on you now: when you finish studying, you begin with a heavy debt and need urgently to find your style and sell.'

This is something Lutz and Guggisberg have clearly not suffered from.

As Lutz jumps on his bike and slides off into the sunset, Guggisberg walks back with us, past an elegant modernist building (a former Siemens' headquarters) and along a peaceful canal, a bit like a tidy maquette of an impressionist landscape. After we say goodbye, we can't help looking at one another and asking ourselves, 'Err, that was Anders, right?'

www.lutz-guggisberg.com
www.galeriefriedrich.ch

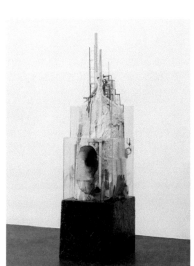

Felsen/Rock, 2011, styrofoam, acrylic glass, plaster, cement, paint, wood, 199 x 50 x 58 cm, courtesy Bob van Orsouw Gallery

Painting is not dead, it only smells funny, 2011, oil and acrylic on canvas, 190 x 240 cm, courtesy Bob van Orsouw Gallery

But humour is something difficult
to talk about; it's like freedom.
Somehow, the more you talk about it,
the more it disappears

Bellevue, Right of the Limmat

The definition 'right of the Limmat' could of course apply to a very large area, but many of the galleries below are clustered around Bellevue, a beautiful area where the Limmat meets the Zurich lake. It is the place to be in the summer months, and no less idyllic in the winter. If you then follow the Limmat (which describes a semi-circle around the city) while remaining on the right side, you will find quiet, leafy neighbourhoods on the hills, where some of the artists in this issue worked in studios which would make many London or New York artists green with envy.

1. AB Gallery

AB in this case stands for Across Borders and this gallery promotes and represents galleries from Islamic Cultures. A good example of the diversity and richness of the art to be found in this highly cosmopolitan marketplace.

Klausstrasse 23
www.ab-gallery.com

2. A/B/Contemporary

An interesting new player in the Zurich scene, with some pretty high-impact shows in its arsenal, such as the complex, and often heart-breaking, political-personal-historical satires of Vietnamese painter Xuan Huy Nguyen (the artist's first exhibition in Switzerland ends on January 14th), or the varied and surprising (it is rare to be able to use that latter adjective without irony in today's art world) paintings, photographs and installations of Swiss duo *Caroline Bachmann & Stefan Banz*.

Breitensteinstrasse 45
www.abcontemporary.com

3. Galerie Bruno Bischofberger AG

Part of a cluster of galleries near Bellevue on the right side of the Limmat. The gallery sells some pretty big paintings by bigger-than-life figures such as George Condo, David Salle and Julian Schnabel and Vladimir Shinkarev.

Utoquai 29
www.brunobischofberger.com

4. Cabaret Voltaire

No tour of Zurich would be complete without a contemplative pause by this landmark of art history and anarchist history, the first floor a noisy cradle of the Dada movement. Recently reopened, the new space hosts exhibitions and events and even includes a shop (selling Freitag bags and other design gadgets) and a lend-

Bellevue, Right of the Limmat

ing library. The feel, however, is more 'tribute band' than 'real deal' – the Dadaist motto, 'protest against the madness of the times', replaced by a more timely 'conform to the silliness of the era – and exit through the gift shop'.

> Spiegelgasse 1
> www.cabaretvoltaire.ch

5. Hammer Gallery Zurich

This gallery happens to be on the left side of the Limmat, but it is worth crossing the bridge over for. The gallery specialises in photographic work and holds strong exhibitions illustrating the variety and richness of the medium at the moment through a highly original list of talent.

> Beethovenstrasse 20
> www.hammergallery.ch

6. Galerie Jamileh Weber

More big names here: Frank Stella, Sean Scully, Joel Schapiro. The gallery also represents the work of seminal Swiss graphic designer and visual artist Karl Gerstner. Early next year the gallery will be showing, among others, works by Jahanguir, Hanspeter Hofmann, Rebecca Horn, Alois Lichtsteiner, Darryl Pottorf and Aldo Rossi.

> Waldmannstrasse 6
> www.jamilehweber.com

7. Kashya Hildebrand

Like the Hammer Gallery, Kashya Hildebrand is located on the left side of the Limmat, by the city centre, offering a central position to art that would often be found at the margins. Since moving from Geneva in 2004, the gallery has been tireless at promoting the work of emerging artists from all kind of backgrounds and working in all kinds media (painting, collage, sculpture, photography and even calligraphy). The list has a strong focus on cultural and national identity, politics and religion. Jung-Yeon Min's show *Nomad* runs to February 4th, and is then followed by *Contemporary Chinese Ink Brush Painting*: Qu WeiWei, Li Yonfei, Jiang Shan Chu, from February 9th to March 24th.

> Talstrasse 58
> www.kashyahildebrand.org

8. Kunsthaus Zürich

One of Switzerland's leading museums, it combines impressive temporary exhibitions with an amazing permanent collection, which includes works ranging from the Swiss Realist tradition, to its exact opposite in the works of John Henry Fuseli and Arnold Böcklin, and works by Félix Vallotton and Fedinand Hodler – all the way down to Zurich Concrete art and Alberto Giacometti (who said the Swiss didn't have an art tradition?). But there's not just Swiss art here, with good collections of Impressionist, Modernist, Constructivist and even Nordic Expressionist works.

> Heimplatz 1
> www.kunsthaus.ch

9. Galerie Lelong

Zurich's base of this international gallery, the New York and Paris home of some of the leading modern art names, from Cildo Meireles and Ana Mendieta to Helio Oiticica and Yoko Ono.

> Ramistrasse 7
> www.galerie-lelong.ch

10. Mai 36

Any gallery tour of Bellevue should finish at Mai 36, one of the big names of the Zurich art scene. The quality of the shows is always high, with artists such as John Baldessari, Peter Hujar, Thomas Ruff, Christoph Rütimann, Paul Thek, Stefan Thiel, Matthias Zinn all having shown in 2011. Koenraad Dedobbeleer runs from January 20th to March 10th, followed by Roe Ethridge.

> Rämistrasse 37
> www.mai36.com

11. Gallery Römerapotheke

If you are in the same area, you must make sure to stop by this gallery, which will regularly come up with surprisingly fresh exhibition choices, such as their recent show with Volker März (pictured) or Marcel Gähler (surprising monochromatic paintings of old curved television screens), the haunting figurative canvases of Marcin Cienski, or the varied and more sculptural works of Alexandre Joly. It's a fascinating space with a friendly and inspiring atmosphere. Jana Gunstheimer runs till January 7th. *Chess Massacre* – 'Zurich vs. Berlin in a hot chess tournament between artists and collectors' – opens on January 13th, alongside KampfKunst, a group show featuring Uros Djurovic, Trevor Guthrie and Florian Heinke.

Rämistrasse 18
www.roemerapotheke.ch

Corinne Güdemann

We meet Corinne Güdemann at her house on one of the leafy hills on the right side of the Limmat. The streets are eerily quiet. Traditional houses rub shoulders with modern apartment blocks and the odd architectural experiment in metal, concrete and wood. It is a sunny morning, with just a bit of mist, and one could easily image oneself to be on the hills of L.A., if it weren't for the slightly stolid look of these rather Germanic bourgeois dwellings and the clockwork efficiency of the tram system. The sounds seem to have been muffled by the mist, and as we walk down that street, we can't help feeling we are walking into a David Lynch movie – something that, as we shall see, is not so far from Güdemann's own work.

Alice in the Trees, 2010, oil on canvas, 160 x 120 cm

The day before, we had just visited another painter, Thomas Mullenbach (see Elephant 10), who lives in a similarly idyllic suburban setting. Both Güdemann and Mullenbach are natural painters. But whereas Mullenbach cultivates a purposeful vagueness in his canvases, working hard to preserve a certain innocence in his gaze – while moving from subject to subject with an ease that is reminiscent to that of a photographer in the William Eggleston fashion – Güdemann, on the other hand, works in diametrically opposite mode, relentlessly attacking her subjects (often the same subject: herself), with targeted strikes. The gaze, here, is never innocent or neutral. One is often catching glimpses of things through branches, or from a not necessarily licit or friendly distance: children playing in the woods, talking in a church, windows lit by tv-sets. Or one is catching the eye of the painter herself, scrutinizing her own face, body, or indeed our own gaze, one voyeur tracking down another.

Güdemann has a painting studio on the ground floor and a drawing studio at the top floor of her house. Both have plenty of light. The windows open to a garden and a beautiful view of Kreis 5. Güdemann arrived in Zurich when she was sixteen years old to attend an Art and Craft School. She studied textile design (an attention to textile patterns and textures is often present in her work) and at the age of twenty-three moved to Vienna, where she studied painting for six years.

When I started painting, still in Switzerland, I was doing figurative work. Originally, I wanted to attend Maria Lassnig's classes, because I had seen her work in an exhibition about Austrian painting and was impressed by her work. She had just started a master class at that time. But when I went there with my drawings, her assistants recommended that I go to Arnulf Rainer's classes. They thought that Maria's teaching was very didactic and probably not free enough for me. So I attended Rainer's classes and changed my style to something more abstract. It was really taboo to paint figuratively at the time! Coming back to Zurich didn't help as nobody was doing this here either. It was more a 'conceptual, neo, geo and so on kind of art'...I had a crisis and decided to come back to that style through *Day's Work*, a series of self-portraits I did in 1994. I went to the studio every day, and every working day I made a self-portrait. There are more than sixty paintings in this series. Each of them has the same format (30x30 cm) and is painted with oils on plywood. It took me quite a while, maybe nine months, as I had a job on the side and couldn't go to the studio freely.

— Somehow, isn't that the equivalent, for a painter, of being a monk in a mountain monastery – trying to look back at oneself in a very reflective way? This was not reflective in a psy-

Gehölz, 2011, oil on canvas, 160 x 120 cm

chological way. The act of painting, of being there and looking at the same time at the same subject, every day, was my main interest. Day by day, painting the same subject was a challenge: for me to undergo the routine and find a fresh way of seeing it, as if for the first time, again and again. If you look at them all, at the same time, it's like a wave: each portrait has its own singularity with small differences like the expressions and the light changing. Returning to figurative work through the surface of things and objects – that was what interested me in this process. And to find out what I really wanted to paint. I think this is why I began first to use my own face, then my own body as a subject. The first series of self-portraits, *Day's Work*, was done with a mirror. But then, I started to work without an instrument. It became more like a lifestyle work. I was drawing what my eyes could see.

Corinne Güdemann

Im Wald, 2010, oil on canvas, 120 x 160 cm

Covering my subjects with shields, barriers, curtains or veils was a way for me to play the game of seeing, watching, or being seen

In painting, and portraiture in particular, the gaze is traditionally male, and dominant – whereas here what we have is clearly something more feminine. Is that something you are conscious of? It is, definitely. When I painted I was very conscious of this phenomenon. I was reading books about female painters. I was interested in how you can project your own ideas on these figures, because they don't confront you – these traditional motives of feminine nudity.

You mentioned the textile design course. And we noticed that you often pay attention to textiles in your work. Was that an influence? I've been asked many times about this... Of course, I can't exclude the fact that somehow there's an influence, but I'm not interested in textiles in a professional way. I actually never worked in that area. But I like the painted structure of textiles, and how the tones of colours develop with light on the materials.

I noticed that you have a series focusing on toys, which seems to be done on plywood. It matches pretty well with the idea of toys, doesn't it? The small paintings are always realized on wood. I like the structure of wood, there's a very good resistance with the brushes and, when included in the painting, it reveals another texture.

Is there a relationship with abstraction, as in this being a way of bringing abstraction back into figurative painting? That's true. It's a way of bringing in another layer, another dimension to the painting, so that it's not too realistic, or not *only* realistic. I'm trying to find a balance between the medium – painting itself – and the meaning of it. It stays figurative, but I try to extend it and make the painting freer. Now the format is also changing – I suppose I'm becoming more emancipated!

At the start of a new cycle, is there always a theme or an idea? There is an idea, but mostly, it's a mixture of pictures I see. Lately, I became interested in 'voyeurism', 'Peeping Tom', but more in the sense of the joy, or the pleasure, of watching, rather than in the purely sexual aspect. As my obsession with watching is quite obvious, I consider myself a voyeur too. Covering my subjects with shields, barriers, curtains or veils was a way for me to play the game of seeing, watching, or being seen. I try to make the subject more interesting, a factual situation more complex. In these last paintings, I have worked with reeds, ponds, a river, and with children, and subsequently, the mystery of their youth. At the end of the day, when you look at the paintings, it's not only harmony or beauty that you feel – it becomes more a question of atmosphere, and the angle of vision. Actually, as you are looking at that scene, you could be the voyeur.

Stille Wasser, 2010, oil on canvas, 160 x 120 cm

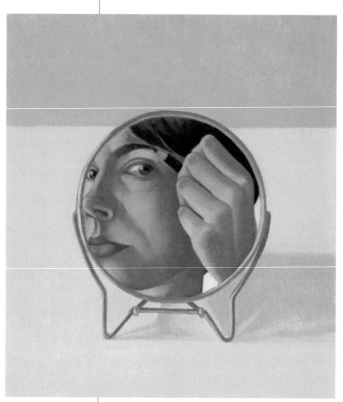

Make Up, 2000, oil on canvas, 4 parts, each 34 x 30 cm

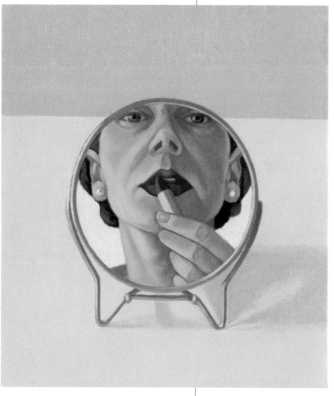

Of course, seeing something in the distance or through trees or reeds creates a sense of drama, suspense... That's what I'm interested in. According to the subject there is always a possibility of making it more mysterious, complex and install a suggestive atmosphere.

The painting *Alice in the Trees*, for example, comes from a photo my husband took of my daughter. It's obviously a reference to *Alice in Wonderland*, and labyrinths, stairs, etc. It's surreal, but not in a Dalí kind of way – it is more in the form of an 'every-day surrealism'. The surrealism comes from how you compose or cut the picture. Playing with elements can completely change one's vision of reality. I sometimes also change the colours of pictures and cut them apart, or change the subject, organizing a new composition with very factual scenes from life. I am interested in the uncanny, the slightly eerie.

Another example of this reorganizing of original pictorial material can be seen at work in Stille Wasser. *The original photograph shows a boy on a rock by a pond. But by cutting most of the boy's body and leaving just his legs, and mixing them with images from other photographs, you have managed to create something far more intriguing and evocative.* [Looking at one of the paintings she has been working on.] This is absolutely a collage. The origin of this painting is photos I have taken by night around the neighbourhood. It's a mixture of pictures that I have put together, in order to find a new composition.

The painting shows a block of flats, seen at night, in winter, from behind a tree. Every room in the block of flats is lit with a different colour, and these reflect differently against the branches of the tree. We are deep in David Lynch territory here. I really saw these colours, and it's so much better than television...

And you like to work on different layers, don't you? Exactly. I like to work and re-interpret my paintings. I don't want them to be too realistic, or photographic, and that's why I try to disturb the composition. I often turn my paintings upside down while working on them, so that provides me with a more abstract view. I'm not scared to have drippings or to throw colours on their surfaces, or even to scratch them. It's also a way of re-interpreting or including them in the scene, in the painting.

We have now moved onto another canvas. The subjects are again seen from a possibly menacing distance. Two young people, a boy and a girl, are chatting in a corner of a church The preponderance of the atmosphere is again pretty strong here. The people you see are my children. They are in a church we visited in Palermo, and there is this man and this confessional chair. The light is playing with the architecture, and it may suggest something strange. What about this male figure, does he represent a danger for this perfectly innocent pair – my son and my daughter? We don't know...

But again, maybe these are just two kids being watched by a caring parent. One of the strengths of your work is the fact that you don't overdo the drama, or the menace. David Lynch is not always around the corner. [Looking at a picture of her son reading a book.] This was a very autobiographical painting, actually. It was the first time that my son Lorenz would read for himself. For me, it was a wonderful emotion that I caught with my camera before painting it.

www.corinneguedemann.ch
www.stephanwitschi.ch

Bürde, 2008, oil on canvas, 160 x 120 cm

Christian   Vetter

Having just had a daughter, Christian Vetter has probably not been getting his full share of sleep, which is maybe why he has a bed on the mezzanine over his studio. His home is also just around the corner, which is convenient, though *convenience* may not be top of his list of creative priorities.

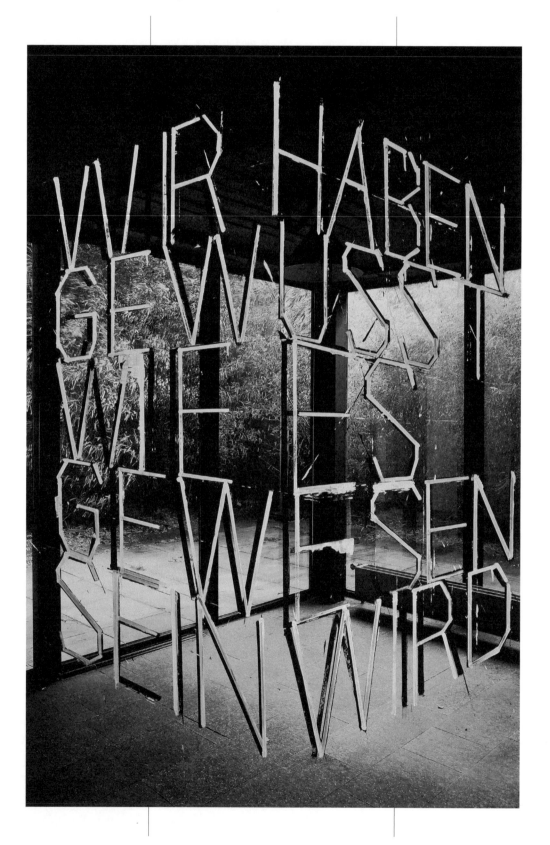

Untitled (part of the series *Wissen Infinitiv*), 2011, acrylics and inkjet-print on paper, 200 x 134 cm

'It's maybe too comfortable to live here. You feel trapped sometimes. I enjoy it when I am in a big city. Here everything is so... *neat*. Even the outskirts... As an artist, I feel inspired when things are not so perfect. All you can see here is a perfect surface. For example, in Mexico [from where he has just come back] the surface is more open and you can see into the structure of things – while they are being built, and collapsing and then being rebuilt – whereas here everything is finished.

'There is a lot of support from the state – that's the good part. The bad part is that it probably makes you a bit lazy. You don't have to fight so hard. Sometimes I think we produce a lot of average things. The motivation to produce something really good is not as strong here. We live disconnected from the rest of the world. We're not even part of Europe.'

Vetter started his career producing abstract expressionist paintings, which, he says, went maybe 'too well'. 'I try to work against some resistance, and I went the other way and tried to paint realistic pictures. It was very interesting in terms of getting to know what an image was, and what my interest in a particular image was, but in terms of painting, it was, well, boring. I would struggle to finish paintings. I felt a very strong discomfort with the whole thing. I knew I had to change something again.'

'In the 90s, in Zurich, it was almost a crime to be a realistic painter. The climate was (and still is) very ideological. I have always questioned these assumptions. Especially if you live here. If you want to do something good for the world, then go out and do it. But not art. That is too easy, and not really appropriate, playing the good guy and telling people what is right and wrong; here – it doesn't mean anything.'

But even if his work is never directly political, politics seems to be always just around the corner. It is difficult not to think of it as being at least militant, and playing heavily with the language of protest. On first encountering his work, one could be forgiven for thinking of a blackboard in an empty classroom where angry students had scrawled their feelings next to the half-effaced left-overs of some convoluted theory.

'I am definitely a political being. But I don't like art that is obviously political. I don't like it when artists preach. But I am interested in the world and maybe I can't help sounding political. I think there's an aggressiveness, or a desperation, in the work. It has become very difficult to do something that has an effect on other people. I think a lot of art has become just a nice product for the art market – I despair about this.

'In recent years, we've had a lot of painting celebrating its own power. But I doubt if things are really like this. I no longer believe in the power of painting as a means to make

Untitled (part of the series Painting Manifesto), 2010, oil on paper, 42 x 60 cm

A lot of art has become just a nice product for the art market — I despair about this

historical work, as, say, in Neo Rauch and a lot of the German school of painting. I believe this is a dead end. They are just repeating empty gestures.'

A turning point in Vetter's career occurred five years ago when he went to Beijing for a six-month studio residency: 'From the very first day there, I just changed everything. I renounced colour, I renounced using photographic references. My painting became less realistic. My work became my own language. It was a moment of great crisis. I had become really fed up with everything. The change didn't have that much to do with China. It just helped to be in such different surroundings. I may have done this if I had stayed here. But it would have taken me longer. It was lucky I could leave everything behind.'

Does he ever think of going back to colour, one cannot help wondering.

'No, I don't miss it at all. I like colour, but I always found it too stressful dealing with colours. It was like a liberation moving away from it.'

Coming back to Switzerland after Beijing was, he says, 'the same shock I always have coming back and realizing that you are living

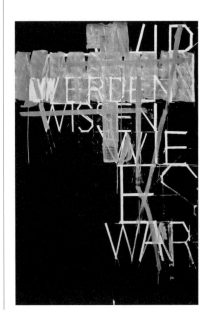

Untitled (part of the series Wissen Infinitiv), 2011, acrylics on paper, 200 x 134 cm

Glag Ship Store, 2011, installation

in a glasshouse. At first, I just forgot everything about Beijing. The memories came back later. Maybe it has to do with the lack of connections between life there and life here.'

In fact, tensions between radically opposite poles – black/white, order/disorder, etc. – are a constant presence in Vetter's work. 'It's always a struggle: between wanting to build something on canvas and realizing the impossibility of doing so. I think that's a vital process.

'I try to understand the complexity of the world, and I believe that is a political act. Not to find quick answers.' And the act of making art is part of this refusal to simplify. At the same time, he tries to be very economical with the means he uses. There are letters and grids on the walls, papers on tables. The studio makes one think of an old-fashioned, pre-computers typography workshop.

'I have been working with words for about a year. I like if paintings are not just self-referential, and language is a good way of reaching outside, something that is not really there. It also has something to do with my conviction that painting is language. I tried to understand how this language is made out. I think about the differences between the literal and the painterly language. I think it is an interesting question: what happens to a word once it becomes a material thing, once it is painted. You feel the meaning evaporates...

'When I started to paint words, I was looking for letters I could easily paint with rulers. I started to use a grid. The letters are adjustable: they can be smaller or thinner, but they follow this grid. I asked a typographer to programme them as a font. We are working on a metafont, which is a system of programming fonts so that letters are defined from the inside, from their structure, rather than shapes – and that is exactly what I am interested in: letters not as specific shapes, but as structures.'

When we ask him about research, he tells us, 'The research is my work. I understand my work as a process of research. It's not as if I did research, and then my work.'

We come onto his *The End* series, which features the phrase 'The End' over a number of works. 'It's quite a pessimistic series. I often feel there is no way to do painting any more. But, on the other hand, I feel that dealing with the end, dealing with the lack of possibilities, is also a way of going on.'

By the end of the series, even the words 'The End' have become illegible, as if even 'The End of Painting' could no longer be expressed in painting.

On the floor, we find a pile of canvases with black & white frames painted on them. The frames are empty – an attempt, according to the painter, to, 'paint the loss of the painting. I called them *Mirrors*. Mirrors who don't reflect any image anymore.

'I have reached a bit a crisis with regards to painting on canvas,' he says, pointing to the large black & white photographic inkjets pinned to the wall. 'I have ordered these today, and I want to start painting words on the images.

'I think my work is not conceptual at all. It just happens. A lot of things that are not planned happen. I think a lot about my work, but then work quite unconsciously. I do something and it often surprises me. Sometimes I even think I am not really the author of my work, but that the work is coming through me in order to become visible. It is like a real experience. I know it sounds a bit esoteric... I do things and I fail a lot, and that's also the motivation to go on.'

www.christianvetter.ch

I try to understand the complexity of the world, and I believe that is a political act

Untitled *(The End)*, 2011, acrylic on paper, 42 x 60 cm

Giacomo Santiago
Rogado

Patrick
Rohner

Jürg
Stäuble

Christine
Streuli

Michel
Verjux

Marcia
Hafif

Dennis
Hollingsworth

Markus
Weggenmann

Duane
Zaloudek

Axel
Lieber

Joseph
Marioni

Joachim
Bandau

Heike Kati
Barath

Francis
Baudevin

Sabina
Baumann

Martin
Mele

Judy
Millar

François
Morellet

Reto
Boller

John
Nixon

Monika
Brandmeier

François
Perrodin

Urs
Frei

Stefan
Gritsch

Katharina
Grosse

Galerie
Mark Müller

Hafnerstrasse 44
CH – 8005 Zürich

T +41 (0)44 211 81 55
F +41 (0)44 211 82 20

mail@markmueller.ch
www.markmueller.ch